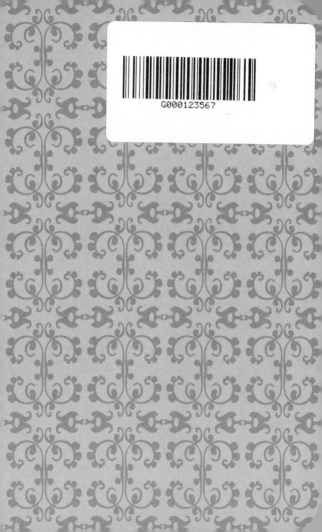

THE LITERARY
POCKET COMPANION

Emma Jones

PAVILION

A Think Book for Pavilion Books

This edition published by Pavilion Books in 2008
First published in the United Kingdom in 2004 by Robson Books
10 Southcombe Street, London W14 0RA

Imprints of Anova Books Company Ltd

Text and design © Think Publishing 2004
The moral rights of the authors have been asserted

Edited by Emma Jones
The Companion team: Vicky Bamforth, James Collins, Charlie Furniss,
Harry Glass, Rhiannon Guy, Lou Millward, Matthew Stadlen,
Jo Swinnerton and Malcolm Tait

Think Publishing
The Pall Mall Deposit
124–128 Barlby Road, London W10 6BL
www.thinkpublishing.co.uk

ISBN 978-1-862058-24-8

2 4 6 8 10 9 7 5 3 1

Printed and bound by Millenium International Printing, China

www.anovabooks.com

THE POCKET COMPANION SERIES:
COLLECT THEM ALL

The Birdwatcher's Pocket Companion
by Malcolm Tait and Olive Tayler
ISBN 978-1-862057-97-5

The Cook's Pocket Companion
by Jo Swinnerton ISBN 978-1-862057-90-6

The Fishing Pocket Companion
by Lesley Crawford ISBN 978-1-862057-92-0

The London Pocket Companion
by Jo Swinnerton ISBN 978-1-862057-94-4

The Sailing Pocket Companion
by Miles Kendall ISBN 978-1-862057-96-8

The Traveller's Pocket Companion
by Georgina Newbery and Rhiannon Guy
ISBN 978-1-862057-91-3

The Walker's Pocket Companion
by Malcolm Tait ISBN 978-1-862057-93-7

The Golfer's Pocket Companion
by Chris Martin ISBN 978-1-862058-23-1

The Wildlife Pocket Companion
by Malcolm Tait ISBN978-1-862058-25-5

The History of Britain Pocket Companion
by Jo Swinnerton ISBN 978-1-862058-22-4

The Gardener's Pocket Companion
by Vicky Bamforth ISBN 978-1-862057-95-1

INTRODUCTION

There are only, it is said, three stories that have ever been written. Boy meets girl. Boy loses girl. Man hunts whale. Everything you ever read or write is no more than a derivation or combination of these.

Well, at last comes the book to give the lie to that theory. Liberally scattered throughout this volume of literary luminaries, novelistic niceties and poetic polemics are more, many more than just three tales. For *The Literary Pocket Companion* tells the stories behind the stories.

And what stories they are. You'll find out more about Dickens and Chaucer, Keats and Amis than their books could ever tell you. It works the other way round, too. You'll also find out more about *Oliver Twist* and *The Canterbury Tales*, 'Ode to a Nightingale' and *Lucky Jim* than their authors could ever tell you.

For *The Literary Pocket Companion* is far more than just a trivia guide (although if you do tuck it down your sock at the next pub quiz, then that tenner is yours). It opens the portals of the wide world of literature, from the pens that scribble it to the libraries that house it, and every painstakingly crafted phrase in between. It will make you laugh, it will raise your eyebrows, and it will draw you even further into the literary minds that have enriched our ages.

Your bookshelf will never be the same.

Emma Jones, Editor

DIGITAL LITERATURE

Just as it is impossible to determine when the wheel was invented or who had the inspiration to suggest that flesh might taste better were it warmed up a little, the exact moment of the ebook's conception is already hotly contested. Some credit Jim Sachs (the inventor of the computer mouse) with this honour, citing the Softbook he developed in his garage in 1995 – from acrylic sheeting and sprinkler tubes – as the giant leap for readers everywhere.

At the same time, however, in the skies above Detroit, Daniel Munyan was furiously making notes. Seeing the discomfort of a fellow passenger who was struggling to angle his reading light, Munyan had a moment of inspiration and dreamt up the Everybook in all its digital literary glory. Both were unaware of the Sony Bookman, a digital reading device launched to little fanfare in the USA in 1992.

Referring both to the digital viewing device itself and the text file, the ebook follows in a long tradition of attempts to condense as much text as possible into the smallest physical space. Whether ebooks succeed where miniature manuscripts and microfiches have failed, however, will depend on their acceptance by the public at large. The co-operation of several high-profile authors, including Dean Koontz and Stephen King, can only help in this respect, as will the proliferation of 'pirated' novel transcripts that can be located easily online and the increasing versatility of mobile telephones and PDAs.

Yet perhaps the biggest challenge for those who wish to replace the print and paper in our lives with microchips and LCD (liquid crystal display) is to develop an ebook viewer that can not only hold 25 novels in its databanks, but which is equally effective at stopping doors and squashing flies.

TAKE A BREAK

Victor Hugo's *Les Misérables* (1862) contains one of the longest sentences in the French language. The author crafted a barely readable 823 words before finally hitting the breathless reader with a full stop.

READING BY NUMBERS

Ten Little Indians, Agatha Christie (1939)
The Nine Tailors, Dorothy Leigh Sayers (1966)
Eight Cousins, Louisa May Alcott (1874)
The Seven Sisters, Margaret Drabble (2002)
Six Characters in Search of an Author, Luigi Pirandello (1921)
Slaughterhouse-Five, Kurt Vonnegut (1969)
The Sign of Four, Arthur Conan Doyle (1890)
Three Men in a Boat, Jerome K Jerome (1889)
A Tale of Two Cities, Charles Dickens (1859)
One Flew Over the Cuckoo's Nest, Ken Kesey (1962)
And Then There Were None, Agatha Christie (1939)

ANAGRAM ANARCHY

Richard Wallace, author of *Jack the Ripper, Light Hearted Friend* (1996), spent years examining what he thought were hidden anagrams in Lewis Carroll's poetry in an effort to prove that the author was the killer. He 'translated' such lines as 'Twas brillig, and the slithy toves/ Did gyre and gimble in the wabe/ All mimsy were the borogoves/ And the mome raths outgrabe' from *Jabberwocky* into such gibberish as 'Bet I beat my glands til/ With hand-sword I slay the evil gender/ A slimey theme; borrow gloves/ and masturbate the hog more!' It's the literary equivalent of playing Ozzy Osbourne LPs backwards and hearing: 'Hi, I'm Satan, how are you?'

AMAZONIAN BOOKSTORES

The world's largest bookshop is the Barnes & Noble Bookstore, New York City, USA. It has over 12 miles of shelving and covers an area of around 14,500 square metres. Waterstones in Piccadilly, London is the largest in Europe, while Amazon.com, with its catalogue of 4.7 million books, is the largest online bookshop in the world.

CHEMICAL FICTION

Rudyard Kipling may have claimed that words are the greatest drug known to man, but legions of other writers have selflessly dedicated themselves to proving him wrong. Here are a few titles to expand your mind as well as your bookshelf...

Alice's Adventures in Wonderland (1865, debated), Lewis Carroll
Cocaine Nights (1996, cocaine), JG Ballard
The Confessions of an English Opium Eater (1821, opium), Thomas de Quincy
The Doors of Perception (1954, mescaline), Aldous Huxley
The Electric Kool-Aid Acid Test (1968, LSD), Tom Wolfe
Fear and Loathing in Las Vegas (1971, anything imaginable), Hunter S Thompson
Glamorama (1998, cocaine), Bret Easton Ellis
Junky (1953, heroin), William Burroughs (under the pen name William Lee)
Kubla Khan (1797, opium), Samuel Taylor Coleridge
Powder (1999, cocaine), Kevin Sampson
The Teachings of Don Juan (1969, mescaline), Carlos Casteneda
Trainspotting (1993, heroin), Irvine Welsh
Under the Volcano (1947, mescaline), Malcolm Lowry

LITERARY FESTIVITIES

When Hay-on-Wye's first secondhand bookshop opened in 1961, it started something of a trend. In this tiny town there are now 39 bookshops for 1300 residents (that's one shop for every 34 people) and a contagious literary hay fever that culminates in late May with the 10-day programme of talks, interviews, lectures, concerts and workshops that is **The Guardian Hay Festival** (www.hayfestival.com).

The Hay has fans in high places: politician and diarist Tony Benn enjoys it so much he once said, 'For me, it has replaced Christmas.' Bill Clinton famously named it the 'Woodstock of the mind' when he was controversially paid to appear in 2001. But no one is completely certain whether he was talking about the meet or the weather – downpours of near Biblical proportions hit the festival every year.

TALES OF THE UNEXPECTED

In *Gulliver's Travels* (1726) Jonathan Swift wrote of 'two lesser stars, or satellites, which revolve about Mars; whereof the innermost is distant from the centre of the primary planet exactly three of his diameters, and the outermost, five; the former revolves in the space of ten hours, and the latter in twenty-one and a half; so that the squares of their periodical times are very near in the same proportion with the cubes of their distance from the centre of Mars; which evidently shows them to be governed by the same law of gravitation that influences the other heavenly bodies'. He had described almost exactly the two moons of Mars more than 150 years before they were discovered.

The Chinese discovered how to make paper in the first century AD. But while they were happy to distribute paper throughout the Asian and Arab worlds, they kept knowledge of its manufacture a closely guarded secret. The news finally got out when an Arab army captured an entire town full of paper makers at the Battle of Talas in 751.

The first words were printed in Chinese temples in the second century AD using engraved marble columns. Pilgrims visiting the temple could print their own Sutras off the columns onto damp pieces of paper.

By the sixth century, Chinese printers had developed engraved wood blocks to print manuscripts. Surviving fragments of Buddhist incantations show this technology had reached Japan in the eighth century, and the world's oldest surviving book, *Jin gang ban ruo bo luo mi jing*, or

The Diamond Sutra, was printed in 868.

In the eleventh century, a Chinese alchemist called Pi Sheng invented movable, reusable type. Pi Sheng's invention was not popular in China and moveable type didn't really take off until Korean King Htai Tjong ordered the first set of 100,000 pieces of type to be cast in bronze in 1403. Nine further fonts were to be developed before Europe discovered typography.

German goldsmith Johannes Gensfleisch zur Laden zum Gutenberg is the father of European printing. He modelled his printing press on wine-pressing techniques and his inks were made from a combination of boiled linseed oil and soot. *The Gutenberg Bibles*, the first mass-produced books and the oldest surviving example of printing with movable metal type, were published on 23 February 1455.

It was only after William Caxton learnt the trade while in Flanders that printing began in England. He established the first English press in Westminster in 1476, and printed *Dictes or Sayengis of the Philosophres*, the first book ever printed in English, in 1477.

In 1534, Henry VIII granted Cambridge University the rights to establish its own press, making it the first printing and publishing house in the world. Its rival, Oxford University Press, is the world's largest university press. Its first book was printed in 1478, only two years after Caxton established his press in Westminster. However, its right to print books wasn't set in stone until 1586.

In 1876, Mark Twain made publishing history when *The Adventures of Tom Sawyer* became the first typewritten manuscript ever to be delivered to a publisher. The typewriter was an 1874 Remington, perfected from Christopher Sholes's 1819 invention.

PULPED FICTION

When engineers started searching for a suitably absorbent pulp to lay on the M6 toll motorway in 2003, they found it at an unexpectedly slushy publishing company. The pulp was needed to strengthen the tarmac and create a long-lasting soundproof layer, and the books they found most suitable were Mills and Boon romantic novels.

About 2,500,000 old copies were pulped and mixed into the road's top layer – that's about 45,000 books for every mile of Britain's first pay-as-you-go motorway. Mills and Boon were chosen because of the books' super-absorbent qualities. 'They may be slushy to many people, but it's their 'no-slushiness' that is the attraction as far as we are concerned,' Brian Kent from Tarmac told the BBC.

11

PUBLISH AND BE DAMNED

Wannabe authors take note! If repeated rejection by publishing houses becomes too much for you to take, you might want to consider self-publishing. You'll have to have a fair amount put aside. A print run that includes project management, critical appraisal, typesetting, ISBN registration, cover design, barcode origination, printing, warehousing and even an optional rewrite service could cost anywhere between £3000 and £8000.

A quick search online yields plenty of companies willing to assist in your literary quest. But, self-publication is only the beginning and without a distribution deal, getting those 1000 newly printed copies of experimental literature onto high-street shelves requires a sharp business sense and a sharper tongue. Sadly, more often than not, such attempts will end in disappointment.

However, it's not all doom and gloom. Take Reverend Graham Taylor of Cloughton, North Yorkshire. Frustrated by successive rejection of *Shadowmancer* – a tale of black magic and Christianity in the seventeenth century – he sold the motorbike he used to visit parishioners and funded its publication at a cost of £3,500. After persuading a major high-street chain to stock copies, his book was spotted and published by Faber UK. A few months later, the book had become a children's bestseller, at which point an American publisher bought the rights for $500,000. There is still no word on whether Reverend Taylor has since replaced his motorcycle.

YOUNG BLOOD

'J' is the youngest letter in the English alphabet. It wasn't added until the 1600s when it grew out of the letter 'i' as its capital form.

HUMP-BACK RIDER

Humping books around can be a tiring business, so spare
a thought for the 400 camels of Abdul Kassem Ismael
of Persia. This tenth-century scholarly grand vizier
never left home without his personal library of
117,000 volumes, and to ensure his librarians could locate
any book almost immediately, the animals were trained
to walk in alphabetical order. It all sheds new light on
Rudyard Kipling's description in the *Just So Stories*
of how the camel got his hump because he spent his days
saying 'humph'.

ON THE ROAD

Books shouldn't be trapped
on overcrowded and
dusty bookshelves nor
reserved for just one reader,
not according to
www.bookcrossing.com at
any rate. They believe our
books should be set free
'into the wild' so they can
spread their joy to all those
who weren't prepared
enough to pack their own
books for the train ride
to work.

US software and internet
guru Ron Hornbaker
founded the organisation in
2001. It already has more
than 250,000 members
'releasing' and 'capturing'
registered books at assorted
locations worldwide. It
works something like this:
you register online (free)
and pick up a code (free),
then after you've finished
your latest catch, you jot
down the code and set it free
(free). The person who picks
it up (free), logs onto the
website (free) and posts you
a lovely message about how
nice it was of you to leave
the book and where they
had last left it (for free).
Bargain.

HOW TO READ

'Begin at the beginning, and go on till you
come to the end; then stop.'

These simple instructions are given by the King of Hearts
to the White Rabbit in Lewis Carroll's *Alice's Adventures
in Wonderland* (1865) when the rabbit is called up to
testify against the Knave of Hearts (who has been accused
of stealing tarts). The King's advice is less nonsensical than
it first seems; the rabbit is reading from a piece of paper
containing verses with no beginning, no end –
and no meaning.

POETIC PUZZLERS

Unscramble these well-known writers
DO HASTY HARM • MY NOBLE RITE •
TOILETS • NO LEGAL PARADE
Answer on page 145.

BOOKSHOP STORIES

Established in 1953 by poet Lawrence Ferlinghetti and
Peter D Martin, City Lights was America's first all-paper-
back bookstore. Based at 261 Columbus Avenue,
San Francisco, the store began its long association with the
writers of the Beat Generation when, in 1955, Ferlinghetti
launched his *Pocket Poets* Series.

In 1956, City Lights fought an obscenity lawsuit for publishing Allen Ginsberg's *Howl and Other Poems*.
Ferlinghetti staked everything on the outcome of the trial.
However, the judge concluded that if a work of art had
social worth (and *Howl*, he argued, did) it couldn't be
classed as obscene. Ferlinghetti left court both victorious
and notorious, the future of City Lights secured.

Mary Higgens Clark, 'America's Queen of Suspense', was paid £45 million for a five-book deal with Simon & Schuster.

A two-book deal with Penguin Puttnam earned **Tom Clancy**, author of *The Hunt for Red October*, £32 million.

HarperCollins paid **Michael Crichton**, creator of *Jurassic Park* and *ER*, £27 million for a two-book deal.

Stephen King received £23 million for his final four-book deal before he announced he was giving up writing.

Barbara Taylor Bradford, author of *A Woman of Substance*, was given £20 million for a three-book deal in 1994.

After the huge success of his American Civil War novel *Cold Mountain*, **Charles Frazier** was paid $8 million for his second book on the basis of a one-page outline. That's a large leap from the $100,000 he was offered for *Cold Mountain* in the mid-1990s.

JK Rowling earned herself an advance of £2 million for the *Harry Potter* series. She was paid just £2500 for the first *Harry Potter* book.

Another £2 million went to **Nicholas Evans** for his first novel, *The Horse Whisperer*, after furious bidding on the manuscript at the Frankfurt Book Fair.

After the success of his best-selling novels *High Fidelity* and *Fever Pitch*, **Nick Hornby** received £2 million for two books on moving to Penguin.

Hari Kunzru received £1.25 million for UK, American and European rights on publication of his debut novel *The Impressionist* in 2002.

The largest amount ever to be given to an unknown author (£700,000) went to **Eoin Colfer** for *Artemis Fowl*, 'the new Harry Potter'.

BOOKS BEFORE THE BIG TIME

It's a rare writer who makes it big on their first book. Here are some of the first offerings of some of our favourite authors...

John Berger, *A Painter of Our Time* (1958)
Angela Carter, *Shadow Dance* (1966)
Wilkie Collins, *Antonina* (1850)
Joseph Conrad, *Almayer's Folly* (1895)
Charles Dickens, *Sketches by Boz* (1836)
George Eliot, *Scenes of Clerical Life* (1858)
F Scott Fitzgerald, *This Side of Paradise* (1920)
EM Forster, *Where Angels Fear to Tread* (1905)
George Gissing, *Workers in the Dawn* (1880)
Thomas Hardy, *Desperate Remedies* (1871)
Jerome K Jerome, *On the Stage – and Off* (1885)
James Joyce, *Chamber Music* (1907)
DH Lawrence, *The White Peacock* (1911)
Iris Murdoch, *Sartre: Romantic Rationalist* (1953)
Sir Walter Scott, *The Lay of the Last Minstrel* (1805)
Robert Louis Stevenson, *An Inland Voyage* (1878)
Bram Stoker, *The Primrose Path* (1875)
Anthony Trollope, *The Macdermots of Ballycloran* (1847)
Herman Melville, *Typee, a Peep at Polynesian Life* (1846)

HOLY COW

You might think that an author tends to write about subjects he knows well. Not so with Oliver Goldsmith, who remarkably chose to write books on subjects of which he happily admitted to knowing nothing. One of these was *The History of the Earth and Animated Nature* (1774), about which Samuel Johnson wrote: 'If he could tell a horse from a cow that was the extent of his knowledge of zoology; and yet [it] can still be read with pleasure from the charm of the author's style'.

LITERARY PRIZES

Hungarian-born American journalist Joseph Pulitzer established the Pulitzer Prize as an incentive to excellence in his 1904 will. Prizes in literature were to go to an American novel, an original American play performed in New York, a book on the history of the United States, an American biography, and a history of public service by the press. Since the prizes were launched in 1917, the judging panel has increased the number of awards to 21 and introduced poetry as a subject in the literature category. The prizes are awarded each April by the President of Columbia University.

Only two winners have turned down the prize: Sinclair Lewis for *Arrowsmith* in 1926 (novel) and William Saroyan for *The Time of Your Life* in 1940 (drama). Lewis refused the prize saying he believed that the Pulitzer was meant for books that celebrated American wholesomeness and his novels, which were critical, should not be considered; Saroyan turned his down saying that art could not be patronised by wealth. At $7500 a pop, he was making a pretty big point.

John F Kennedy is the only US President to be awarded a Pulitzer Prize. He was presented with the 1957 Pulitzer Prize in Biography for *Profiles in Courage*.

GHOST DUSTERS

The dust jacket has been hanging around book covers for centuries, but Lewis Carroll can be thanked for its present form. He came up with the very sensible idea of printing the title of *The Hunting of the Snark* (1872) on the spine of the jacket so it could be easily found on a bookshelf.

AVOID CLICHÉS LIKE THE PLAGUE

The fact of the matter is that the passage of time has driven a nail into the coffin of the carefully crafted words of a select few. In a nutshell, and not to mince words, the following have taken the bull by its horns to stand head and shoulders above the rest...

Cloudcuckooland
Aristophanes (c.444 BC –380 BC), *Birds*. The word (in its closest rendition from Greek to English) comes up as a suggestion for the name of the capital city of birds.

All hell broke loose
John Milton, *Paradise Lost* (1667)

The law is an ass
Charles Dickens, *Oliver Twist* (1837–1838)

Boys will be boys
Anthony Hope, *The Dolly Dialogues* (1894)

The female of the species is more deadly than the male
Rudyard Kipling, 'The Female of the Species' (1911)

Every dog has his day
George Borrow, *Lavengro* (1851)

'Tis better to have loved and lost than never to have loved at all
Tennyson, *In Memoriam* (1850)

Funny peculiar or funny-ha-ha?
Ian Hay, *The Housemaster* (1936)

A dark horse
Benjamin Disraeli, *The Young Duke* (1831)
When originally used, it applied literally to a dark horse which had unexpectedly won a race: 'A dark horse which had never been thought of... rushed past the grandstand in sweeping triumph.'

That's the long and short of it
WS Gilbert, *Princess Ida* (1884)
Most probably influenced by Shakespeare's 'the short

and the long of it', spoken by Mistress Quickly in *The Merry Wives of Windsor*.

As fresh as [is] the month of May
Geoffrey Chaucer, *The Canterbury Tales, Prologue* (c.1387)

I'm no angel
Although some consider it to have originated with Mae West, it was actually first used by Becky Sharp in William M Thackeray's *Vanity Fair* (1848)

No time like the present
Mrs Manley, *The Lost Lover* (1696)

So near and yet so far
Tennyson, *In Memoriam* (1850)

Variety is the spice of life
William Cowper, *The Task* (1785)

Ignorance is bliss
Thomas Gray, *Ode on a Distant Prospect of Eton College* (1742)

Thanks for nothing
From 'Thank you for nothing', Cervantes, *Don Quixote* (1605)

BRIGHT YOUNG THINGS

In 1979, *The Observer* published a list of 80 young people they predicted would define the country's culture, politics and economics for a generation. They repeated the exercise in 2004; these are the few writers who made the final cut:

Hari Kunzru (novelist)
Martin McDonagh (playwright)
Alice Oswald (poet)
Helen Walsh (author)
Sarah Waters (novelist)
Louise Welsh (author)

BOOKS TO BAWL TO

Read'em and weep...

After You'd Gone, Maggie O'Farrell (2000)
The Amber Spyglass, Philip Pullman (2000)
A River Runs through It, Norman MacLean (1976)
Doctor Zhivago, Boris Pasternak (1957)
Flowers for Algernon, Daniel Keyes (1966)
Gone with the Wind, Margaret Mitchell (1936)
Jane Eyre, Charlotte Brontë (1847)
Little Women, Louisa May Alcott (1868)
The Lovely Bones, Alice Sebold (2002)
Rebecca, Daphne du Maurier (1938)
Sophie's Choice, William Styron (1979)
The Tin Drum, Günter Grass (1959)
Watership Down, Richard Adams (1972)
The World According to Garp, John Irving (1978)

CREATIVE COCK-UPS

If Herman Melville ever wondered why the first edition of his novel *Moby-Dick* (1851) failed to sell well in Britain, he needed look no further than the last page. His all-important conclusion – you know, that little bit about Ishmael surviving the attack of the white whale – had been mislaid in transit, leading reviewers to slam the book for its hasty and unsatisfactory conclusion, and readers to throw their books down in despair at the unhappy tale.

WHAT'S THAT WORD?

The word 'lethologica' describes the state of not being able to remember the word you want.

LOST IN TRANSLATION

Book titles that don't work so well in the 21st century...

American Bottom Archaeology (Anon, 1983)

The Big Book of Busts (John Watson and Eric Schiller, 1994)

British Tits (Christopher M Perrins, 1979)

Enid Blyton's Gay Story Book (Enid Blyton, 1957)

Flashes from the Welsh Pulpit (J Gwnoro Davies, 1889)

Games You Can Play With Your Pussy (Ira Alterman, 1885)

Alterman can also be thanked for: *Sex Manual For People Over 50, Do Diapers Give You Leprosy?, Games for the John* and *A Man in the Hand is Worth Two in the Bush.*

The Hookers' Art (Jesse A Turbayne, 1993)

How to Mount Deer for Profit or Fun (Archie Phillips, 1980)

'Invisible Dick' the boy superhero in *Sparky* (1960)

The Romance of the Beaver (A Radclyffe Dugmore, 1914)

Scouts in Bondage (Boy Scouts Association, 1930)

The Scrubber Strategy (Baviello, Bowie and Beerman, 1982)

Shag the Caribou (C Bernard Rutley, 1943)

Whippings and Lashings (Girl Guide Association, 1970)

POETIC PUZZLERS

**Four writers joined by one furtive theme.
Name the link...**

Ian Fleming • Grahame Greene
Christopher Marlowe • W Somerset Maugham

Answer on page 145.

HOW TO READ

Every extreme has its opposite, and speed-reading is no exception. The 'Slow Reading Movement' (much like the 'Slow Food Movement' except that it aims to decrease the speed of your eyes rather than that of your mouth) is the advocate of savouring the written word at a more leisurely pace.

The currently underground movement (it presumably takes a bit of time to read the manifesto) traces the idea back to the words of Nietzsche, who wrote of the idea of 'teaching slow reading' in the preface to *Daybreak* (1881): 'In the midst of an age of "work", that is to say, of hurry, of indecent and perspiring haste, which wants to "get everything done" at once, including every old or new book: this art does not so easily get anything done, it teaches to read WELL, that is to say, to read slowly, deeply, looking cautiously before and aft, with reservations, with doors left open, with delicate eyes and fingers.'

The cause offers a great excuse for not finishing the novel that's been sat on your bedside table since last Christmas, but you might look pretty simple staring at the same page for half an hour on the train to work.

A READING RAINBOW

Red Badge of Courage – Stephen Crane (1895)
A Clockwork Orange – Anthony Burgess (1962)
Chrome Yellow – Aldous Huxley (1921)
How Green was my Valley – Richard Llewellyn (1939)
The Blue Bird – Maeterlinck (1909)
The Indigo Children – Lee Carroll and Jan Tober (1999)
Prater Violet – Christopher Isherwood (1945)
The Rainbow – DH Lawrence (1915)

THE REWRITE WAS BETTER

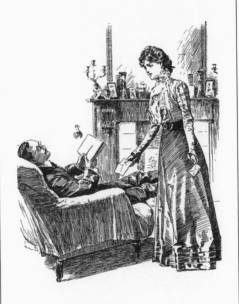

The Importance of Being Furnished
Oscar Wilde pokes fun at the cushions and attitudes
of well-to-do nineteenth-century England.

ORIGIN OF THE TITLES

If you were asked where John Steinbeck took his inspiration for *The Winter of Our Discontent*, you'd probably know the answer (Shakespeare, *Richard III*), but what about the following 'adopted' titles:

Far from the Madding Crowd, **Thomas Hardy**
From *Elegy Written in a Country Churchyard*
by Thomas Gray
'Far from the madding crowd's ignoble strife
Their sober wishes never learned to stray.'

Cakes and Ale, **W Somerset Maugham**
From Shakespeare's *Twelfth Night*, Act II, scene iii
'Sir Toby Belch: Dost thou think, because thou art
virtuous, there shall be no more cakes and ale?'

For Whom the Bell Tolls, **Ernest Hemingway**
From 'Meditation XVII – No Man is an Island'
by John Donne
'...any man's death diminishes me, because I am involved
in mankind; and therefore never send to know for whom
the bell tolls; it tolls for thee.'

The Darling Buds of May, **HE Bates**
From the Shakespeare sonnet
'Shall I compare thee to a summer's day?
Thou art more lovely and more temperate.
Rough winds do shake the darling buds of May
And summer's lease hath all too short a date.'

Of Mice and Men, **John Steinbeck**
From *To a Mouse* by Robert Burns
'The best laid schemes o'mice an' men, Gang aft a-gley'

Brave New World, **Aldous Huxley**
From Shakespeare's *The Tempest*, Act V, scene i
'Miranda: How beauteous mankind is! O brave new world
That has such people in't!'

The Power and the Glory, **Graham Greene**
From the Bible, Matthew 6:9
'For thine is the kingdom, and the power,
and the glory, for ever, amen.'

The Sound and the Fury, **William Faulkner**
From Shakespeare's *Macbeth*, Act V, scene v
'Macbeth: It is a tale
Told by an idiot, full of sound and fury,
Signifying nothing.'

CEASE THIS DETESTABLE BOO-HOOING INSTANTLY!

As befitting an author who penned an entire play on the pleasures of bringing correct English phonetics to the masses, George Bernard Shaw left a bizarre will bequeathing his worldly goods to the development of a rational spelling system, which wasn't resolved until 1999, almost half a century after his death. The will, which named the National Gallery in Dublin, the Royal Academy of Dramatic Art, and the British Museum as beneficiaries of the remaining fortune, prompted decades of parliamentary debates, threats of legal action, and discord between the organisations, which weren't to receive a penny until the English language was reformed.

When an out-of-court settlement awarded a one-off payment towards a book on phonetic spelling, the dispute appeared settled until the British Library got in on the act. They argued that it was the library (which had split from the museum in 1972) that was Shaw's intended beneficiary, since he had acknowledged in his will 'the incalculable value to me of my daily resort to the reading room of the institution at the beginning of my career'. The quarrel was finally resolved in 1999 when the two agreed to share the £7 million inheritance.

The 'Wicked Bible'

In a fifteenth-century edition of the King James Bible, the word 'not' was accidentally omitted from the seventh commandment, so that it actually encouraged readers to commit adultery. The copies were recalled immediately (dashing the hopes of many).

The 'Fool's Bible'

A 1632 print-run made a similar boob. They replaced 'no' with 'a' in Psalm 14 to read: 'The Fool hath said in his heart there is a God.' The resulting fine put the printing house out of business.

The 'Unrighteous Bible'

The word 'not' was also omitted in a later 1653 edition, but this time in Corinthians VI to read: 'Know ye not that the unrighteous shall inherit the Kingdom of God', much to the consternation of all do-gooders.

The 'Printer's Bible'

In a 1702 version, the printing house must have been aware of the ramifications of error. They substituted the word 'printers' for 'princes' in Psalm 119 to read: 'printers have persecuted me'.

The 'Sinner's Bible'

Ten years later and an Irish edition was commanding the faithful to 'sin on more', replacing the 'sin no more' that is generally preferred by practising Christians.

The 'Murderer's Bible'

The word 'murmurers' was replaced with 'murderers' in an 1801 print-run. 'Let the children first be killed' (for 'filled'), it bloodthirstily continued.

The 'He Bible'

A 1923 edition more than stated the obvious when it got the sexes mixed up: 'A man may not marry his grandmother's wife', it sternly advised.

THE NATION'S FAVOURITE POEMS

**As voted by the British public for National Poetry Day`
in 1995**

1. *If*, Rudyard Kipling
2. *The Lady of Shalott*, Alfred Lord Tennyson
3. *The Listeners*, Walter de la Mare
4. *Not Waving But Drowning*, Stevie Smith
5. *The Daffodils*, William Wordsworth
6. *To Autumn*, John Keats
7. *The Lake Isle of Innisfree*, WB Yeats
8. *Dulce et decorum est*, Wilfred Owen
9. *Ode to a Nightingale*, John Keats
10. *He Wishes for the Cloths of Heaven*, WB Yeats

A 30-YEAR RIDDLE

'Why is a raven like a writing desk?'
'I haven't the slightest idea'

The Mad Hatter puts forward both this riddle and its lack of an answer at his tea party in Lewis Carroll's *Alice's Adventures in Wonderland* (1865). It caused so much frustrated conjecture that 30 years later, Carroll published the following solution in the preface to the 1896 edition: 'Because it can produce a few notes, tho they are very flat, and it is never put with the wrong end in front!' However, in 1976, Carroll-admirer Denis Crutch pointed out that in the original preface, Carroll had actually written: 'It is nevar put with the wrong end in front' (raven spelt backwards), which had been mistakenly corrected by proofreaders.

GONE WITH THE WIND

After 50 years of speculation, the mysterious death of children's author and aristocratic adventurer Antoine de Saint-Exupéry finally came a step closer to being resolved when traces of his Lockheed Lightning P-38 turned up in the Mediterranean near Marseilles in 2004. The writer of dreamy classic *The Little Prince (Le Petit Prince)* had vanished without a trace on 31 July 1944, during an Allied reconnaissance mission, with some even claiming that he'd headed back to the Sahara to hook up with the book's time-travelling hero. As the evidence seems to suggest the crash was an accident, the news might well prompt a name change for the Aéroport Antoine de Saint-Exupéry in his home town of Lyon.

LITERARY PHOBIAS

Scared of reading or saying long words? Then you possibly suffer from (but will probably never be able to read or say) 'hipomonsteresquipedalophobia', the phobia of long words. Other linguistic phobias include 'graphophobia', the fear of looking at writing, 'sophophobia', the fear of learning (a likely story) and 'verbophobia', the fear of words.

POETIC PUZZLERS

**Four writers joined by one chugging theme.
Name the link and the titles...**

Agatha Christie • Michael Crichton
Graham Greene • E Nesbit

Answer on page 145.

TAKE ME TO YOUR LEADER

No suspension of disbelief was required on Halloween, 30 October 1938. The US radiolistening public fell for it hook, line and sinker when the cool, calm voice of Orson Welles boomed out through the speakers to tell an alarmed nation that the aliens had landed and that they hadn't come in peace. It may seem hard to believe today, but the first airing of the radio version of HG Wells' *The War of the Worlds* caused such widespread panic that the police headquarters in Trenton, close to the fictional scene, recorded an onslaught of calls: 'Between 8:30pm and 10pm received numerous phone calls as result of WABC broadcast this evening re: Mars attacking this country. Calls included papers, police depts including NYC and private persons... At least 50 calls were answered. Persons calling inquiring as to meteors, number of persons killed, gas attack, military being called out and fires. All were advised nothing unusual had occurred and that rumors were due to a radio dramatization of a play.'

Welles appeared apologetic before the assembled press the next morning (although he later took full credit for the play's effect in a BBC interview in 1955), but writer HG Wells was seething. The script was such a loose adaptation of the original that Wells demanded a retraction ('Or I will blast you with my deadly heat-ray gun,' were apparently not his words).

THUMBS UP FROM THE VATICAN

Lew Wallace's *Ben Hur* (1880) was the first piece of fiction ever to be blessed by a pope.

YOU ARE HOW YOU READ

The four classes of reader according to Samuel Taylor Coleridge:

• **Sponges,** who absorb all that they read and return it in nearly the same state, only a little dirtied.
• **Sand-glasses,** who retain nothing and are content to get through a book for the sake of getting through the time.
• **Strain-bags,** who retain merely the dregs of what they read.
• **Mogul diamonds,** equally rare and valuable, who profit by what they read, and enable others to profit by it also.

MOONSHINE

The moons of all the planets are named after Greek gods, except those of Uranus. In this case, characters in Shakespeare plays and Alexander Pope's *The Rape of the Lock* are the inspiration. Uranus has five larger moons (Miranda, Ariel, Umbriel, Titania and Oberon), 11 smaller moons (Cordelia, Ophelia, Bianca, Cressida, Desdemona, Juliet, Portia, Rosalind, Belinda, Puck and one still to be named) and five irregular moons (Caliban, Sycorax, Setebos, Stephano and Prospero).

ONCE THEY WERE LIBRARIANS

John Braine • Casanova
Jane Gardam • David Hockney
Sir Ludovic Kennedy • Philip Larkin
August Strindberg • Laurie Taylor
Mao Tse-Tung

DEEP THOUGHT

In 1997, a group of Cambridge scientists studying the age of the universe found that they had been beaten to the answer by cult novel *The Hitchhiker's Guide to the Galaxy* (1995). In Douglas Adam's sci-fi classic, an alien race programmes a computer called Deep Thought to study the universe to find the ultimate meaning of life; it returns, seven-and-a-half million years later, with the result, 42. It was the same answer that scientists calculated 15 years later after no fewer than three years working on 'The Hubble Constant' (an equation that puts the age of the universe at 23 billion years). That's science fiction for you.

BOOKS THAT BECAME SONGS

1984 – David Bowie
Journey to the Center of the Earth – Rick Wakeman
Rime of the Ancient Mariner – Iron Maiden
Wuthering Heights – Kate Bush
And Then There Were None – Exodus
Romeo and Juliet – Dire Straits
Brave New World – Donovan
Lord of the Flies – Iron Maiden
Blake's Jerusalem – Billy Bragg
For Whom the Bell Tolls – Metallica
Tom Sawyer – Rush
Bell Jar – The Bangles
War of the Worlds – Jeff Wayne
All Quiet on the Western Front – Elton John
On the Road – John Denver
Catcher in the Rye – Clandestine

PAPERBACK SAINTS

St Christopher...bookbinders
St Francis de Sales............................authors and journalists
St John of God...booksellers
St John Bosco...editors
St Jerome...librarians
SS David and Celia...poets
SS John of God, Augustine of Hippo.....................printers

D IS FOR DORD

For five years, *Webster's New International Dictionary* famously included an entry for 'dord', a word that does not exist. It was listed between entries for 'Dorcopsis' (a genus of small kangaroo of Papua) and 'doré' (golden in colour), as a noun describing density in the fields of physics and chemistry.

It was a particularly eagle-eyed editor who first aroused suspicions in 1939. He noted that the word was lacking the normal etymological description and searched through the files to track it down. What he found instead was a small card bearing the notation 'D or d, density', which should have been added to the abbreviation section, but had somehow mistakenly turned up in the 'words' pile instead.

'As soon as someone else entered the pronunciation, dord was given the slap on the back that sent breath into its being' explained Philip Babcock Gove, editor-in-chief in 1954. 'Whether the etymologist ever got a chance to stifle it, there is no evidence. It simply has no etymology. Thereafter, only a proof-reader had final opportunity at the word, but as the proof passed under his scrutiny he was at the moment not so alert and suspicious as usual'. That's one editorial team who found itself abbreviated to 'D or k, dense'.

THE REWRITE WAS BETTER

Lord of the Jives
A group of shipwrecked Scots decide who will be ruler
of the island in a Gaelic dance-off. Ralph wins and
is crowned Lord of the Jives; Piggy loses and is killed
in a group riverdance.

UNRAVELLING THE CODE

Handy acronyms for second-hand book purchasing on e-bay...

ARC	Advance reader's copy (paperback edition circulated before the trade edition for publicity)
AUTO	Autographed
EXLIB	Ex-library book
F/E	First edition
HB/DJ	Hardback with dust jacket
HIC	Hole in cover
SC	Slight crease
NC	No cover
NM	Near mint
OOP	Out of print
PB	Paperback or paperbound
PC	Poor condition
RC	Reader copy (a book in a good condition but with no real investment value)
ROM	Romantic
VHTF	Very hard to find
WOC	Writing on cover

And one that should be there:

DBAWOI Don't believe a word of it

ABOUT A B

Some of our best-loved writers prefer a double initial approach, but what do the AA, the DH or the TS stand for?

WH Auden – Wystan Hugh
JM Barrie – James Matthew
AS Byatt – Antonia Susan
ee cummings – Edward Estlin
Edward Estlin has become known as
'the poet who never uses capitals'.
GK Chesterton – Gilbert Keith
TS Eliot – Thomas Stearns
EM Forster – Edward Morgan
AE Housman – Alfred Edward
PD James – Phyllis Dorothy
DH Lawrence – David Herbert
CS Lewis – Clive Staples
He actually preferred to be called Jack
JB Priestley – John Boynton
JK Rowling – Joanne Kathleen
JD Salinger – Jerome David
JRR Tolkien – John Ronald Reuel
HG Wells – Herbert George
PG Wodehouse – Pelham Grenville
WS Gilbert – William Schwenk
AA Milne – Alan Alexander
The illustrator of the *Winnie the Pooh* series
is another double-barreller:
EH Shepard – Ernest Howard

THE DEVIL'S DICTIONARY

Nineteenth-century American satirist Ambrose Bierce offers his sardonic views on the writing habit...

BLANK-VERSE, *n.* Unrhymed iambic pentameters – the most difficult kind of English verse to write acceptably; a kind, therefore, much affected by those who cannot acceptably write any kind.

DICTIONARY, *n.* A malevolent literary device for cramping the growth of a language and making it hard and inelastic. This dictionary, however, is a most useful work.

DRAMATIST, *n.* One who adapts plays from the French.

ELEGY, *n.* A composition in verse, in which, without employing any of the methods of humor, the writer aims to produce in the reader's mind the dampest kind of dejection. The most famous English example begins somewhat like this:

The cur foretells the knell of parting day;
The loafing herd winds slowly o'er the lea;
The wise man homeward plods; I only stay
To fiddle-faddle in a minor key.

GRAMMAR, *n.* A system of pitfalls thoughtfully prepared for the feet for the self-made man, along the path by which he advances to distinction.

NIHILIST, *n.* A Russian who denies the existence of anything but Tolstoy. The leader of the school is Tolstoy.

NOVEL, *n.* A short story padded. A species of composition bearing the same relation to literature that the panorama bears to art. As it is too long to be read at a sitting the impressions made by its successive parts are successively effaced, as in the panorama. Unity, totality of effect, is impossible; for besides the few pages last read all that is carried in mind is the mere plot of what has gone before. To the romance the novel is what photography is to painting. Its distinguishing principle, probability, corresponds to the literal actuality of the photograph and puts it distinctly into the category of reporting; whereas the free wing of the romancer enables him to mount to such altitudes of imagination as he may be fitted to attain; and the first three essentials of the literary art are imagination, imagination and imagination. The art of writing novels, such as it was, is long dead everywhere except in Russia, where it is new. Peace to its ashes – some of which have a large sale.

PLAGIARIZE, *v.* To take the thought or style of another writer whom one has never, never read.

PROOF-READER, *n.* A malefactor who atones for making your writing nonsense by permitting the compositor to make it unintelligible.

QUOTATION, *n.* The act of repeating erroneously the words of another. The words erroneously repeated.

REALISM, *n.* The art of depicting nature as it is seen by toads. The charm suffusing a landscape painted by a mole, or a story written by a measuring-worm.

RIME, *n.* Agreeing sounds in the terminals of verse, mostly bad. The verses themselves, as distinguished from prose, mostly dull. Usually (and wickedly) spelled 'rhyme'.

ROMANCE, *n.* Fiction that owes no allegiance to the God of Things as They Are. In the novel the writer's thought is tethered to probability, as a domestic horse to the hitching-post, but in romance it ranges at will over the entire region of the imagination – free, lawless, immune to bit and rein.

STORY, *n.* A narrative, commonly untrue.

WITTICISM, *n.* A sharp and clever remark, usually quoted, and seldom noted; what the Philistine is pleased to call a 'joke'.

THE REAL EPICS

• The world's longest nonfiction work is *The Yongle Dadian*, a 10,000-volume encyclopaedia produced by 5000 scholars during the Ming Dynasty in China 500 years ago.

• The 2000-year-old *Mahabharata*, the 'Great Epic of India', could well be the world's largest book in poetic form. It began at 24,000 couplets and has gradually expanded to just over 100,000.

• The longest novel is Marcel Proust's *Remembrance of Things Past*. The 13-volume work contains a total of 9,609,000 characters, with each letter and space counting as one character.

• The world's largest book is known to be *The Golden Book of Cleveland*. It measures five feet by seven feet, contains 6000 pages for signatures and weighs about two and a half tonnes.

• The longest spoken epic in the world is the Tibetan story *King Gesser*. The 20-million-word tale takes six hours to recite.

• The longest poem was written by prolific Indian Poet Nikhil Parekh. *Only as Life* measures a herculean 1470 lines, 1100 stanzas and 7900 words.

• The longest dictionary is the *Oxford Dictionary of National Biography*, a 60,000-page compilation of 60 volumes that would take up a full 11 feet on your bookshelf.

FINDING YOUR WAY AROUND

Most libraries use the Dewey Decimal Classification (DCC system), which works to the following classifications:

000–099 *General Works*
199–199 *Philosophy*
200–299 *Religion*
300–399 *Social Studies*
400–499 *Languages*
500–599 *Science*
600–699 *Technology*
700–799 *Fine Arts*
800–899 *Literature*
900–999 *History and Geography*

SORTES VERGILIANAE

There's magic to be found in books and not just in the plot. *Sortes vergilianae* is an ancient method of divining the future based on the 'magic' of Virgil's poetry. Fate is dealt by opening the book at a random page and identifying a line by three throws of the dice. The Roman Emperor Hadrian is said to have consulted the *sortes vergilianae* in an effort to inquire into his future, and many, including St Jerome, believed that Virgil's fourth *Ecologue* (which was written around 41 or 40 BC) predicted the birth of Christ.

It may sound like hocus pocus, but things took a decidedly coincidental twist when the King of England Charles I conjured up his fortune in 1642. Virgil provided the following prophetic line: 'May he be harried in war by audacious tribes and exiled from his own land'. Just seven years later, Oliver Cromwell fulfilled the poet's prophecy by relieving Charles of his head.

PRINT-RUN RECORD

Book five of the Harry Potter series holds the record for the largest print run in history. Thirteen million hardback copies of *Harry Potter and Order of the Phoenix* were printed to meet the huge demand generated for its release, which saw 875,000 advance orders taken on Amazon.com alone. *Harry Potter and the Goblet of Fire* (book four) holds the record for the most advance orders; a colossal 5.3 million copies (that's around 40 times as many as the average bestseller) were ordered and prepaid worldwide before its release.

LITERARY GAMES AND LINGOS

The Glass Bead Game (Hermann Hesse, 1943)

Played out in the futuristic post-Holocaust land of Castalia, Hesse's Glass Bead Game – an ancient symbolic language game – demands a mastery of music, mathematics, philosophy and logic if it is to be understood. Presided over by the Magister Ludi, it is used to interpret and predict social development, and its dictates are treated with the gravest reverence in Castalia and beyond.

Undaunted by the fact that Hesse does not provide a comprehensive list of symbols or rules of play for his hypothetical language, several societies have sprung up since the book's publication determined to play the game and use their readings for good. We can only wish them luck!

POETIC PUZZLERS

Four writers joined by one cinematic theme.
Name the link and the films...
JG Ballard • Robert Harling • Stephen King • Irvine Welsh
Answer on page 145.

LITERARY PRIZES

The British Poet Laureate fulfils a variety of functions: the holder of the post is the realm's official poet (and accepted into the royal household) with tasks that include writing verses for court and national occasions. Once chosen by the British reigning monarch from a list of nominees, the post is awarded and accepted for life.

The ceremony takes its name from the Latin *laureatus* ('crowned with laurel'), which derives from the ancient Roman tradition of honouring excellence in poetic achievement.

So far there have been 19 Poets Laureate. The first was Edmund Spenser. He fulfilled the role from 1591 to his death in 1599 despite the fact that the first folio edition of *The Faerie Queene* wasn't published until 10 years after his death.

The current Poet Laureate is Andrew Motion. He accepted the role in 1998.

The longest-serving Poet Laureate was Alfred Lord Tennyson. He held the post for 42 years from 1850 until his death in 1892.

The shortest-serving Poets Laureate were Thomas Shadwell (1642–1692) and Nicholas Rowe (1674–1718), both of whom quit their posts after only three years.

The oldest Poet Laureate was John Masefield (1885–1977). He was 92 when death ended his 37-year reign. The oldest to accept the post was William Wordsworth: he picked up the title at the age of 73.

The youngest was Laurence Eusden, who became Poet Laureate at the age of 30.

John Dryden was the only Poet Laureate to be dismissed from the post. He was sacked for not taking an oath of allegiance to William III.

Quentin Blake became the first Children's Laureate in 1999. Ann Fine replaced him in May 2001.

NEW WRITING DEFINITIONS

An anonymous posting on the internet and a work of sheer brilliance...

Autobiography Car maintenance manual.

Copyright 'This is okay to copy, right?'

Ghost writing The number of books, articles, stories that you have written in your head but are yet to commit to paper.

Headline Wrinkly bits on forehead caused by writing deadlines.

Lead What you use to walk your dog while formulating new ideas.

Love scene Said when you finally write a good paragraph: 'I love that scene'.

Playwright Play computer Solitaire 90% : write 10%

Procrastination An oxymoron because it begins immediately after you land an assignment.

Publicution When a critic pans your book in their newspaper review.

Referfence When an interviewee falls through so you replace them with your neighbour.

Science faction Science fiction writing for the unimaginative.

Womanuscript Feminine of manuscript.

LITERARY RECLUSES

Probably the literary world's most famous recluse, **JD Salinger** went into hiding in the hills of New Hampshire after his debut novel *The Catcher in the Rye* (1951) became a massive success.

Nobel Laureate **JM Coetzee** didn't show up to collect either of his Booker Prizes.

Don DeLillo rarely gives readings and keeps interviews to a minimum. He once handed over a piece of paper inscribed with the words: 'I don't want to talk about it,' so he wouldn't even have to voice his answer.

Loner **John Fowles**, author of *The French Lieutenant's Woman*, despised literary pomp and was notoriously uneasy around other writers considering them 'vain' and self-serving. He lived in self-imposed exile in one of the wildest spots of the South Coast.

Thomas Harris courteously refuses all enquiries from journalists with the words: 'I really can't start giving interviews now.' He also rejects all editorial suggestions on his writing.

Thomas Pynchon, author of *Gravity's Rainbow* and *V*, is so publicity-shy he once dived out of an apartment window in Mexico City to escape a photographer. He ran away into the mountains, where he hid long enough to grow a moustache and gain the local nickname 'Pancho Villa'. According to one legend, he is actually JD Salinger.

WHAT'S IN A NAME?

William Faulkner's name is actually spelled 'Falkner'. The printer who set up his name for his first book misspelt it (adding the 'u') and Faulkner decided to live with the new name rather than bother to correct his editor.

EKERS AND GUSHERS

Flaubert was an 'eker'. Intent on finding the right word ('le mot juste'), he rarely squeezed out more than a paragraph a day.

Samuel Johnson wrote *Rasselas* in one week to raise money to pay for his mother's funeral. He sold it to a publisher for £100 without even reading it over once.

Louisa May Alcott authored *Little Women* in two-and-a-half months. The resulting sales pulled her out of poverty.

Dame Barbara Cartland was one of the world's most gushing authors; even in her 80s, she was writing an average of 23 books a year. In her 77-year career, she managed to churn out over 700 books.

Enid Blyton was without doubt the most prolific children's writer of the twentieth century. By the time of her death in 1968, she had also become the most published author of all time with over 700 books and 10,000 short stories to her name.

Harold St John Hamilton (Frank Richards) wins the award for the most words ever written. The author who created *Billy Bunter* put around 75 million to paper.

Taking the crown from Enid Blyton, Brazilian **Jose Carlos Ryoki di Alpoim Inoiue** became the most prolific novelist of all time when he published 1058 novels between 1986 and 1996 – that's more than 105 a year.

POETIC PUZZLERS

In Dostoevsky's *The Idiot*, who was the idiot?
Answer on page 145.

THE REWRITE WAS BETTER

Reader, I carried him.

THE REWRITE WAS BETTER

Finnegan's Cake
James Joyce charts the story of a publican near
Dublin, his wife, their three children and the pies
and pastries they serve.

CREATIVE COCK-UPS

Long-winded writer Marcel Proust received a rejection
letter from French publishing house Fasquelle with the
words: 'My dear fellow, I may be dead from the neck up, but
rack my brains as I may, I can't see why a chap should need
thirty pages to describe how he turns over in bed before going
to sleep.' When the novel, *Remembrance of Things Past*, was
subsequently published, this passage hadn't been cut.

THE TITLE, THE TITLE AND NOTHING BUT THE FULL TITLE

The full titles of books often better known by their shortened forms

The Fortunes and Misfortunes of the Famous Moll Flanders, Daniel Defoe (1722)

The History of Tom Jones, a Foundling, Henry Fielding (1749)

The Life and Opinions of Tristram Shandy, Lawrence Sterne (1759–1767)

The Life and Strange and Surprising Adventures of Robinson Crusoe, Daniel Defoe (1719)

The Posthumous Papers of the Pickwick Club, Charles Dickens (1837)

The Strange Case of Dr Jekyll and Mr Hyde, Robert Louis Stevenson (1886)

Three Men in a Boat (To say Nothing of the Dog), Jerome K Jerome (1889)

Through the Looking Glass ...and what Alice Found There, Lewis Carroll (1871)

The Alchemist: A Fable About Following Your Dream, Paulo Coelho (1995)

LITERARY LINGOS

Lapine (*Watership Down* – Richard Adams, 1972)
If Richard Adams is to be believed, amid the warrens of the idyllic English countryside much is being said. Lapine – spoken by Hazel and friends – is an intricately conceived, yet beautifully simple naming language with its own vocabulary and a fully realised grammatical framework.

TOP BIDDERS

Exceptional prices paid at Christie's...

World Auction Record for a seventeenth century book – US$6,166,000 (New York, 2001) First folio edition of *Comedies, Tragedies & Histories*, William Shakespeare (1623)

World Auction Record for a manuscript – US$30,802,500 (New York, 1994) *Codex Hammer*, Leonardo da Vinci

World Auction Record for an illuminated manuscript – £8,580,000 (London, 1999) *Book of Hours, The Rothschild Prayer Book* (1505)

World Auction Record for any printed book – US$8,802,500 (New York, 2000) The Birds of America, from *Original Drawings*, John James Audubon

World Auction Record for an incunable – £4,621,500 (London, 1998) *The Canterbury Tales*, Geoffrey Chaucer (1476 or 1477). The book was one of the first major works printed in England by William Caxton, in 1477.

World Auction Record for a Bible – US$5,390,000 (New York, 1987) *The Gutenberg Bible*

World Auction Record for a medical book – US$1,652,500 (New York, 1998) Charles V's coloured copy of *De humani corporis fabrica libri septem*, Andreas Vesalius (1543)

World Auction Record for a children's book – US$1,542,500 (New York, 1998) Suppressed first edition of *Alice's Adventures in Wonderland*, Lewis Carroll (1865)

ONE AND A HALF FOOT

Derived from the Latin *sesquipedalis* (literally, a foot-and-a-half long), the word 'sesquipedalian' is used to describe the size or the use of long words. It was passed down by the Roman poet Horace, who mentions *sesquipedalia verba*, or 'foot-and-a-half-long words', in *Ars poetica* ('the art of poetry'). Fittingly, the word itself provides some of the longest sesquipdalians: writers who use long words are described as sesquipedalianists; their style of writing is sesquipedalianism, the habit of using them is sesqui-pedality, and a hyperpolysyllabicsesquipedalianist is some-one who takes pride in their use of really long words.

LITERARY LATIN

acte est fabula – the play is finished

ars gratia artis – art for art's sake

ex libris – from the library of

index librorum prohibitorum – list of forbidden books

lector benevole – kind reader

literati – men of letters

magnum opus – the greatest piece of work (of an artist)

ps (post scriptum) – written later

theatrum mundi – the theatre of the world

ubi supra – where (cited) above

v.l. (varia lecto) – variant reading

WHAT TO READ WHERE

Africa
A Good Man in Africa, William Boyd
The Famished Road, Ben Okri
A Year in Marrakesh, Peter Mayne
Out of Africa, Karen Blixen
Heart of Darkness, Joseph Conrad

Australia
The Songlines, Bruce Chatwin
Oscar and Lucinda, Peter Carey
Promised Lands, Jane Rogers
A Fringe of Leaves, Patrick White

China and Hong Kong
Wild Swans, Jung Chang
Shanghai Baby, Wei Hui
Kowloon Tong, Paul Theroux

France
Notre Dame de Paris, Victor Hugo
My Father's Glory, Jean de Florette and *Manon des Sources*, Marcel Pagnol

India
A Passage to India, EM Forster
Kim, Rudyard Kipling
The God of Small Things, Arundhati Roy
Midnight's Children, Salman Rushdie
The Age of Kali: Indian Travels and Encounters, William Dalrymple

Ireland
Echoes, Maeve Binchy
Portrait of the Artist as a Young Man, James Joyce

Italy
The Talented Mr Ripley, Patricia Highsmith
The Leopard, Giuseppe Tomasi di Lampedusa

Japan
Shogun, James Clavell
Memoirs of a Geisha, Arthur Golden
An Artist of the Floating World, Kazuo Ishiguro
The Wind-Up Bird Chronicle, Haurki Murakami

Russia
Eugene Onegin: A Novel in Verse, Alexander Pushkin
Crime and Punishment, Fyodor Dostoevsky
Anna Karenina: A Novel in

Eight Parts, Leo Tolstoy
Doctor Zhivago, Boris Pasternak

News of a Kidnapping, Gabriel Garcia Marquez
Rayuela, Julio Cortazar

Spain
Death in the Afternoon, Ernest Hemingway
As I Walked Out One Midsummer Morning, Laurie Lee

US
Absalom, Absalom!, William Faulkner,
To Kill a Mockingbird, Harper Lee
Washington Square, Henry James
The Catcher in the Rye, JD Salinger

South America
The Fruit Palace, Charles Nicholl

THE POWER OF THREE

Three Blind Mice – Agatha Christie (1950)
The Three Clerks – Anthony Trollope (1858)
Three Guineas – Virginia Woolf (1931)
Three Hostages – John Buchan (1924)
Three Men in a Boat – Jerome K Jerome (1889)
Three Men on the Bummel – Jerome K Jerome (1900)
(also known as *Three Men on Wheels*)
The Three Musketeers – Alexandre Dumas (1844)
The Three Sisters – Anton Chekhov (1901)

WHERE DO YOU READ?

A survey of 1000 British people for Bedtime Reading Week 2002 found the most popular place to read was in bed (65% of readers). 25% liked to relax with a book in the bath, 10% preferred to take a book to the toilet (mainly men), almost half liked to read on holiday and a third read on the journey to work. More than a third said they wished they had more time to read.

TEXTUAL HEALING

In July 2002, the National Reading Campaign commissioned a survey of adult reading habits. Here's what they found…

• Ninety-six per cent of readers surveyed had read something in the past week whether books, magazines, newspapers or text messages (which apparently counts as reading).

• Reading material varied according to age: 70% of 16–24-year-olds had read a magazine, compared to 59% of 55–64-year-olds; 33% of 16–24-year-olds had read fiction, compared to 43% of 55–64-year-olds.

• Nearly half the adults had read five books or more in the previous 12 months, with almost one in five claiming to have read 20 books or more.

• A quarter of adults had not read a book at all during the same period, including almost half of males aged between 16 and 24.

• Two out of five adults had read a book after tips from friends; 16% followed recommendations from colleagues.

FLYING HIGH

Toy company Mattel offered children a less than innocent experience in 2001 when they launched the Harry Potter Nimbus 2000. A toy replica of the broomstick used by Harry Potter in the film version of *Harry Potter and the Philosopher's Stone*, the Nimbus 2000 comes complete with grooved stick, handle for easy riding, magical swooping and wooshing sounds and, to enhance the excitement, the vibrating effects that have made it a top-seller in the nation's sex shops. It seems JK Rowling had a point when she said the Harry Potter series wasn't just for children.

THE TAMING OF THE LEWD

Victorian to the core, English editor Reverend Thomas
Bowdler attacked his editions of Shakespeare, Chaucer
and Gibbons with a prudish red pen believing that
nothing 'can afford an excuse for profanity or obscenity;
and if these could be obliterated, the transcendent genius
of the poet would undoubtedly shine with more uncloud-
ed lustre'. The result – the severe cutting of everything
he considered to be indecent or indelicate – became
known as 'bowdlerising'. Bowdler also 'cleaned up'
Tennyson's *The Wreck of the Hesperus*, substituting such
offensive terms as 'bull' with the explanation
'gentleman cow'.

WRITERS AND THEIR MUSES

If you think it's only the modern celebrity that chases the
wrong skirt (or trousers), think again; authors have been
dipping their pens in forbidden inkwells for centuries…

A young **Lord Byron** was in love with his cousin,
Mary Chaworth, but unfortunately for him she spurned
his attentions.

WB Yeats was romantically involved with Maud Gonne
until she married Major John Macbride in 1903.

Franz Kafka had a stormy relationship with Felice Bauer,
to whom he was engaged (and disengaged) twice in five years.

Edgar Allan Poe lived with his aunt and her 13-year-old
daughter Virginia, whom he subsequently married.

The fact that **Percy Bysshe Shelley** was married did not
stop him running off with Mary Wollstonecraft, who later
authored *Frankenstein* (1818). He was a leading exponent
of 'free love' and although he eventually married Mary in
Paris, he hadn't actually bothered to divorce his first wife.

Oscar Wilde was imprisoned for his affections towards
young blood Alfred 'Bosie' Douglas.

COMMA SENSE

*'the nowing ones complane of my book the fust edition
had no stops I put in a nuf here and thay may peper
and solt it as they please'*

So complained Timothy Dexter when he reissued *A Pickle
for the Knowing Ones* (1802), a 24-page pamphlet,
which had been originally published without once using
capital letters, full stops, commas or any other form
of punctuation. There was, however, one small catch:
rather than add it to the text, the author had simply
added another page at the end containing nothing but
punctuation. His contemporaries scoffed, but Dexter had
the last laugh – the book is now a rare collector's item.

TOP TEN ODD BOOKS

Stéphane Mallarmé wrote 'everything in the world exists
to end up in a book'; it seems he wasn't wrong...

The Unconscious Significance of Hair (George Berg, 1951)
How to Boil Water in a Paper Bag (Anon, 1891)
Teach Yourself Alcoholism (Meier Glatt, 1975)
How to Become a Schizophrenic (John Modrow, 1992)
Nuclear War: What's in it for you? (Ground Zero War
Foundation, 1982)
A Pictorial Book of Tongue Coating (Anon, 1981)
Fish Who Answer the Telephone (YP Frolov, 1937)
The Thermodynamics of Pizza (Harold J Morowitz, 1991)
Who's Who in Barbed Wire (Anon, 1970)
Hand Grenade Throwing as a College Sport
(Lewis Omer, 1918)

WHAT THE DICKENS?

If you thought the death of Krook in *Bleak House* was the result of an over-active imagination, you may be mistaken. There were around 30 cases of 'spontaneous human combustion' on record when Dickens was researching the death for *Bleak House* and (just to prove it isn't the naïvety of Victorian medicine), there have been another 200 non-fiction reports since.

One of the most famous cases occurred in St Petersburg, Florida in 1951. One 67-year-old Mary Hardy Reeser 'spontaneously combusted' while sitting in her easy chair and was found the next day in a blackened circle four feet in diameter. All that remained was a few blackened seat springs, a section of her backbone, a shrunken skull the size of a baseball, and one foot encased in a black slipper just beyond the four-foot circle. The police report declared that Mrs Reeser went up in smoke when her highly flammable rayon-acetate nightgown caught fire, perhaps because of a dropped cigarette, but as the rest of the apartment somehow managed to come through unsinged, nobody is entirely sure.

LAW STORY

Ernest Hemingway was once sued by a 70-year-old Cuban fisherman named Miguel Ramirez, who claimed that Hemingway's Pulitzer Prize-winning novel, *The Old Man and the Sea* (1952), was an unauthorised biography. The wily sea captain's not-altogether-convincing case centred around his assertion that he had spent four days chasing and catching a magnificent marlin in his youth, only to have it eaten by sharks as he towed it back to shore. The suit was thrown out after just a few minutes of thrashing around.

THE OPRAH EFFECT

Every time Oprah Winfrey features a new book in her TV-show book club, it rises in the bestseller list. The club had already created 48 bestsellers when it was temporarily disbanded in 2002, and since its relaunch in 2003 with a new focus on classics, books such as *East of Eden* by John Steinbeck, and *Anna Karenina* by Leo Tolstoy have shot to the top of bestseller lists in the US. The Pevear-Volokhonsky translation of *Anna Karenina*, for example, went straight to number one on the New York Times book list within one week of being featured on Oprah's show. Penguin has already returned to press twice to cater for the growing demand, which has seen 900,000 copies sold since May 2004, compared to the 60,000 copies which had been bought since the book's US release in 2001. Who says television kills reading?

LITERARY FESTIVALS

The intellectual heart of the August Edinburgh Festival, the **Edinburgh International Book Festival** (August, www.edinburghfestivals. com) has been running for over 20 years. It started off as a biennial festival in 1983, becoming annual in 1997 and is now home to over 600 events during its fortnight run. Claiming to be 'the world's leading book festival', it certainly is one of the most intimate with talks and question-and-answer sessions held in a series of makeshift marquees in Charlotte Square.

A Wail of Two Kitties
Two kittens warble their way through solitary
confinement during the French Revolution.

THE ANGRY HOSHIBUDOU

Many an expression is lost in translation from English, but you'd expect the title of a novel to be converted with a fair bit of time and attention. Not so for John Steinbeck's *The Grapes of Wrath*, whose title (taken from the song 'The Battle Hymn of the Republic'), was translated into Japanese as 'the angry raisins'. John Steinbeck's widow was the first to pick up on the schoolboy error on a trip to Japan in 1989 to celebrate the 50th anniversary of the publication of the book. An especially appreciative fan dropped the clanger: 'We like your husband's work very much, particularly *The Angry Raisins*.' Apparently he would have been crushed.

A TWIST OF LEMON

Alcohol has been the inspiration for many a writer...

A Drink With Something In It (1935) –
Ogden Nash (on the benefits of a Martini)

Hangover Square (1941) – Patrick Hamilton

The Ordeal of Gilbert Pinford (1957) – Evelyn Waugh
(based on hallucinations caused by alcohol and sleeping
tablets)

The Power and the Glory (1974) – Graham Greene
(his 'whiskey priest' chooses alcohol over God)

Under the Volcano (1947) – Malcolm Lowry
(considered by Stephen Spender to be one of the best
accounts of a 'drunk' in fiction: 'Lowry shows us how
a drunk thinks and feels, walks and lies down, and we
experience not only the befuddledness of drinking
but also its moments of translucent clairvoyance.')

Anything by Jack Kerouac, Dylan Thomas, Philip Larkin
and Lord 'gin-and-water is my inspiration' Byron.

SPELLING IT OUT

Literacy facts from the National Literacy Trust...

• According to the *CIA World Fact Book*, the UK adult population is 99.6% literate. It estimates that there are 802 million illiterate adults in the world, two thirds of whom are women.

• When literacy is tested in practical situations, more adults perform poorly in the UK than in many other industrialised societies. Twenty-three per cent of UK adults have problems at the lowest level, compared to Sweden, where it is only 7%. Ireland is 1% worse-off than the UK, the USA 1% better.

• Of those who have problems, 93.2% have difficulty with spelling and 39.8% with writing. When tested 68% of the population misspelt accommodation, including 53% of graduates.

• In the 2002 Literacy in the Age of Information report, Britain ranked 16th out of 22 in tests of quantative literacy (understanding figures and statistics), 15th out of 22 in tests of document literacy (understanding how to fill out forms) and 13th out of 22 in tests of prose literacy (understanding newspapers and stories). The countries who ranked lower than the UK were Hungary, Poland, Slovenia, Portugal and Chile.

• Surveys of literacy attainment have been carried out in the UK since 1948. Their main finding is that literacy standards have changed very little in that time.

LITERARY PICK 'N' MIX

Literary collaborations that could have been:

Gone with the Wind in the Willows (Mitchell/ Grahame)
Mole, Ratty and Badger struggle to defend their beloved riverside plantation from being ravaged during the Civil War. Toad, however, doesn't give a damn.

The Dice Man who Mistook his Wife for a Hat (Rhinehart/Sacks)
A psychiatrist treats his seriously disturbed patients based on the random dictates of a die with hilarious and harrowing results.

Brave New World According to Garp (Huxley/Irving)
The bastard son of Jenny Field consumes daily grams of soma to fight his terminal depression.

The Quiet American Psycho (Greene/Easton Ellis)
High-flying, murderous and psychopathic Genesis fan flies to Vietnam to take on a well-intentioned mission of political enlightenment.

On the Road to Welville (Kerouac/Coraghessan)
Colonic irrigation for motorcyclists.

Band of Brothers Karamazov (Ambrose/Dostoevsky)
Inexplicably fighting for the US Army in World War Two, the Karamazov brothers have little time to mull over the other's moral stance and consequently get on fabulously.

Quiet Flows the Don Quixote (Sholokhov/Cervantes)
Sholokhov seeks to correct the unfavorable image of the Don Cossacks by following the adventures of Don Quixote of La Mancha and his faithful squire, Sancho Panza, as they travel through twentieth century Russia.

Stupid White Men are from Mars, Women are from Venus (Moore/Gray) Intolerable self-help guide made even more intolerable by the self-congratulatory political posturing.

NO PLACE UNDER THE TOME

He wasn't the first to sleep at his library desk, but he was certainly the first to move in. In 2004, a homeless New York student said he slept for seven months in a university library without being caught because he couldn't afford his housing costs on top of his tuition fees. The underground life of Steve Stanzak in the Bobst Library on New York's Washington Square – including all the gory details about where he washed and kept his clothes and books (surely on the shelves) – can be read in all its glory on www.homelessatnyu.com.

WHAT'S A 'BOOK'?

Stating the obvious it may be, but UNESCO certainly felt the book needed to be defined in 1950 when they qualified it as 'a nonperiodical literary publication containing 49 or more pages, not counting the covers'. The word itself derives from the Latin 'liber', which originally described the thin peel found between the bark and the wood that was used to jot down notes before the era of parchment. The English word comes from 'bog', the Danish for book, which itself is derived from the name of their bark of choice, birch.

QUOTE UNQUOTE

He who lends a book is an idiot.
He who returns the book is more of an idiot.
Arab Proverb

PC PRONOUNS

In an article published in January 1912 by *The Chicago Tribune*, educational reformer and suffragist Ella Flagg Young proposed the use of alternative gender pronouns to make the English language less biased against women. Editors everywhere would have been grateful if she had devised something elegant and useful; but as her suggestions were his'er, he'er, him'er and his'er's, the alternatives, sadly, were doomed never to catch on.

Young wasn't the first to tackle the issue of gender-neutral pronouns; around 80 new terms have been suggested since the 1850s, but none have made any visible headway in popular usage. In 1884, the composer Charles Converse's proposals (thon and thons) made their way into several unabridged dictionaries, but they were dropped soon after. 'Sie', 'hir', 'ey', 'zie' and 'hesheit' met similar fates.

THE BEST WRITER FOR THE JOB

The Able Coincidence – JN Chance (1969)

Alpine Plants of Distinction – A Bloom (1968)

Anatomy of the Brain – WW Looney (1932)

Criminal Life – Superintendent J Bent (1891)

Crocheting Novelty Pot-holders – L Macho (1982)

Common Truths from Queer Texts – Reverend J Gay (1908)

Electronics for Schools – RA Sparkes (1972)

Grace of God – A Lord (1859)

Inside Story – A Dick (1943)

The Principles of Insect Philosophy – VB Wigglesworth (1939)

Spices from the Lord's Garden – Reverend EID Pepper (1895)

A Treatise on Madness – W Battie MD (1758)

Violence Against Wives – Emerson and Russell Dobash (1979)

The World of My Books – IM Wise (1954)

POET'S CORNER

Part of the south transept of Westminster Abbey, Poet's Corner, contains the tombs and monuments of many of Britain's most distinguished authors, playwrights and poets...

Geoffrey Chaucer
Chaucer was the first to be buried in the Abbey but he wasn't buried here for his literary accomplishments: he was Clerk of Works to the palace of Westminster.

Edmund Spenser
Spenser was the second: his burial started the tradition of burying poets, writers and playwrights near each other in the Abbey.

Rudyard Kipling • Richard Brinsley Sheridan
Samuel Johnson • Thomas Hardy • John Dryden
Alfred Lord Tennyson • Robert Browning
John Masefield • Samuel Johnson • Charles Dickens

Although they are not actually buried here, there are also memorials to Lord Byron, William Shakespeare, John Milton, William Wordsworth, Thomas Gray, John Keats, Percy Bysshe Shelley, Robert Burns, William Blake, TS Eliot and Gerard Manley Hopkins; and writers such as Samuel Butler, Jane Austen, Oliver Goldsmith, Sir Walter Scott, Charlotte, Emily and Anne Brontë, Henry James and Sir John Betjeman.

GONE WITH THE WIND

Three novels have been credited with sales of over 30 million, all of them by American female authors. The top best-sellers are *Gone with the Wind* (1936) by Margaret Mitchell, *To Kill a Mockingbird* (1960) by Harper Lee and *Valley of the Dolls* (1966) by Jacqueline Susann.

EVEN HARRY POTTER WON'T DO

When Scottish teenagers were asked about their reading habits in 2000 by the Organisation for Economic Co-operation and Development (OECD), the results were astonishing. A third of teens said they 'never' or 'hardly ever' read for pleasure, a fifth considered reading 'a waste of their time', and 40% said they only read if they had to. The figures emerged from an international study of 15-year-olds from across 28 countries, which fortunately also revealed that Scottish pupils were in the top six in the international reading literacy rankings. The findings also showed that teen Scots were much more likely to read magazines or newspapers than they were to read books – with 80% claiming to have read newspapers at least several times in the last month.

LITERARY PRIZES

The Booker Prize, the most prestigious award available to British novelists, has secured the fame and fortune of many a previous winner – not least the 2002 victor Yann Martel for the *Life of Pi*. Any novel written by a citizen of the United Kingdom, the Republic of Ireland, or the British Commonwealth is eligible to enter and win the £50,000 prize as long as it is published in the English language and first released in the United Kingdom. The 1981 award winner, Salman Rushdie's *Midnight's Children*, currently holds the title for the 'Booker of Bookers'; it was named the outstanding Booker winner of the first 25 years of the competition in 1993.

HELP WITH HOBBIES

Creative activities worth considering...

The Art and Craft of Pounding Flowers: No Paint, No Ink, Just a Hammer! (Laura Martin, 2001)

The Great Pantyhose Crafts Book (Edward Baldwin, 1982)

Woodcarving with a Chainsaw (Lyn Mangan, 1998)

Lightweight Sandwich Construction (JM Davies, 2001)

More Tea Bag Folding (Tiny van der Plas, 2001)

Original Tricks with Cigars (Micky Hades, 1927)

Pranks with the Mouth (Anon, 1879)

Explosive Spiders and How to Make Them (John Scoffern, 1881)

Levitation for Terrestrials (Robert Kingsley Morison, 1977)

Collect Fungi on Stamps (DJ Aggersberg, 1997)

Let's Make some Undies (Marion Hall, 1954)

How to Cook Husbands (Elizabeth Stong Worthington, 1899)

One Hundred and Forty-one Ways of Spelling Birmingham (William Hamper, 1880)

Play With Your Own Marbles (JJ Wright, SW Partridge, c.1865)

PUB FICTION

Chaucer's pilgrims begin their journey from **The Tabard** in Southwark in his *Canterbury Tales*. His wasn't a literary creation; the popular coaching inn existed until 1873.

Shakespeare's Falstaff often drank at **The Boar's Head** in Eastcheap in the City of London. The Boar's Head actually existed, although it was knocked down in 1830 to make way for the new London Bridge road.

Mary Ann Sailors and grandson Sinbad keep **The Sailor's Arms** in Dylan Thomas' *Under Milk Wood*. It's always open – the clock has been stuck at 11.30pm for the last 50 years.

In Oliver Goldsmith's *She Stoops to Conquer*, Tony Lumpkin can be found drinking in **The Three Jolly Pigeons**.

Miss Abbey Potterton keeps **The Six Jolly Fellowship Porters** in Limehouse in Dicken's *Our Mutual Friend*.

The family of Jim Hawkins keep an inn called **The Admiral Benbow** in Robert Louis Stevenson's *Treasure Island*.

George Orwell first described **The Moon under Water** in an essay in the *Evening Standard* (1946). The name has since been adopted for a chain of pubs operated by JD Wetherspoon.

THE FIVE FATHERS

Daniel Defoe – Father of Modern Prose Fiction
Henry Fielding – Co-Father of the English Novel
Ben Jonson – Father of Poets
Edgar Allan Poe – Father of the Detective Story
Samuel Richardson – Co-Father of the English Novel

GAOL BOOKS

Great literature to have emerged from behind bars...

In the Belly of the Beast: Letters from Prison
Jack Henry Abbott (1981)
A powerful book that became all the more notorious after Abbott committed another murder shortly after his early release.

The Pilgrim's Progress,
John Bunyan (1684)
Imprisoned over long periods for preaching without a licence, Bunyan had plenty of time to think this one up.

Letters and Papers from Prison, Dietrich Bonhoeffer (1951)
Imprisoned for his part in a plot to assassinate Hitler, Bonhoeffer spent his time creating this crucial work of modern theology.

The Prince Machiavelli (1513)
Machiavelli conceived this royal tome after he had been wrongly imprisoned for fomenting a rebellion against Florence's ruling Medici family.

Our Lady of the Flowers Jean Genet (1949)
Notorious French thief and male prostitute, Genet spent most of his youth in prison putting this novel to paper.

On the Yard, Malcolm Braly (1967)
A frightening insight into a US penitentiary by a former inmate of San Quentin.

Don Quixote, Miguel de Cervantes (1615)
Banged up for his debts, Cervantes may have conceived of this classic as a route to financial freedom.

De Profundis, Oscar Wilde (1905)
Wilde is often mistakenly thought to have penned *The Ballad of Reading Gaol* when he was inside it for two years. What he actually created was this miserable tale of a life gone wrong.

MORE MONKEY, WITH LESS ART

A million monkeys, a million typewriters, and sooner or later a simian will have bashed out the scripts for any one of Shakespeare's plays, according to the Infinite-Monkey Theorem that is. First popularised by astrophysicist Sir Arthur Eddington, and then featured by Russell Maloney in his short story *Inflexible Logic*, the idea was also featured in *The Hitchhiker's Guide to the Galaxy*, when an infinite number of monkeys ambush the crew for their opinion on the monkey's script for *Hamlet*. The online Monkey Shakespeare Java Simulator (http://user.tninet.se/~ecf599g/aardasnails/java/Monkey/webpages) sets the current record at 16 letters.

POETIC CRIB

Meter works through recurrent regular stressed and unstressed syllables. The four standard types of strong and weak stresses (known as feet) are...

Iambic – light syllable, then stressed syllable
The cur – few tolls – the knell – of par – ting day.
Thomas Gray, 'Elegy Written in a Country Churchyard'

Anapestic – two light syllables, then stressed syllable
The Assyr – ian came down – like a wolf – on the fold.
Byron, 'The Destruction of Sennacherib'

Trochaic – stressed syllable, then light syllable
There they – are, my – fifty – men and – women.
Robert Browning, 'One Word More'

Dactylic – stressed syllable, then two light syllables
Eve, with her – basket, was – deep in the – bells and grass.
Ralph Hodgson, 'Eve'.

LITERARY CAMOUFLAGE

Female authors who hid their sex

Acton, Currer and Ellis Bell – Anne, Charlotte
and Emily Brontë
The Brontës used these pseudonyms in their first published
work – a joint volume of verse entitled *Poems by Currer,
Ellis and Acton Bell* – but soon revealed themselves after
suspicions that the Bell pennames concealed but
one author.

Isak Dinesen – Baroness Karen Christentze Blixen,
author of *Out of Africa*

George Eliot – Mary Ann (later Marian) Evans

PD James – Phyllis Dorothy James White

Harper Lee – Nelle Harper Lee

George Sand – Amandine-Aurore Lucille Dupin

Even today female authors hide their sex; JK Rowling's
publishers allegedly used her initials on the book cover
because they didn't think boys would buy a book
by a woman.

THE BORROWER

Unpack the books holed up in your attic and you're sure to
find the odd 'misplaced' library book or two, but have you
ever thought about taking them back? Wary of fines, most
hastily return them to the shelves, but not so Ernie
Roscouet who, in 2004, returned a book to a library in
Malta 42 years too late. Expecting a massive fine or even
imprisonment, Roscouet was presented with an altogether
different reaction – a cup of tea, as a reward.

WISE WORDS

Literature with a spiritual point

John Bunyan ....*Pilgrim's Progress*
Teresa of Avila...*The Life of Saint Teresa of Avila By Herself*
Lao Tzu ....*Tao Te Ching*
Prince Siddhartha Gautama ....*The Dhammapada*
Confucius ....*The Analects*
Mother Julian of Norwich ....*Revelations of Divine Love*
Paulo Coelho......*The Alchemist: A Fable About Following Your Dream*
James Redfield ....*The Celestine Prophecy*
Richard Bach ....*Jonathan Livingston Seagull: A Story*

LITERARY PRIZES

The award every writer doesn't want to receive, the Bad Sex in Fiction Award, celebrates just that – the worst examples of sex scenes in contemporary literature. The 2003 prize (presented by the allegedly highly sexed singer Sting) was awarded to Indian writer Aniruddha Bahal for a scene in *Bunker 13* involving a woman who has a swastika shaven into her pubic hair. Among the nominees were Hollywood director Alan Parker, Conservative politician Iain Duncan Smith and authors Paul Theroux, Paolo Coelho and John Updike.

The prize was launched in 1994 when Philip Hook set the standard with the following scene in *The Stonebreakers*: 'Their jaws ground in feverish mutual mastication. Saliva and sweat. Sweat and saliva. There was a purposeful shedding of clothing.' Winners receive a box of cigars for their efforts.

WRITER WHIMS

Ernest Hemingway stood when he wrote, preferably in a pair of oversized loafers, with the typewriter and the reading board chest-high opposite him.

Robert Frost preferred to write while sitting in an armchair.

Charles Dickens always slept facing towards the North because he thought that it would improve his writing. He also used to touch everything three times for luck.

Lewis Carroll wrote most of his books, including *Alice's Adventures in Wonderland*, while standing up. He composed the tale when sitting down – in a boat with the family of the Dean of Christ Church college, Oxford, including 10-year-old daughter, Alice.

Truman Capote would only ever write on yellow paper.

Balzac believed that in order to write a great book he needed to remain chaste. Every time he spent the night with a woman, he would say to himself: 'There goes another masterpiece.'

Roald Dahl wrote his best-loved works in a specially designated writing hut in his orchard.

French novelist **Colette** didn't just read in bed, she preferred to write there too. To make things all the more comfortable, she invented a 'bed-raft' in her Paris apartment on which she slept, ate, entertained, phoned, read and wrote.

WHEN DO YOU READ?

In 2004, World Book Day commissioned a survey of reading habits by profession. Here's what they found...

• Accountants are the biggest readers, spending an average of five hours and 15 minutes a week on their preferred authors (Jane Austen and JRR Tolkien). They tend to do most of their reading during the commute to work.

• Secretaries came second with just under five hours a week. They also like Jane Austen, but tend to do most of their reading in bed.

• Politicians came a close third (also just under five hours). Half preferred histories while 47% opted for biographies – Betty Boothroyd's *Don't Call Me Madam* was the favourite at the time of the poll.

• Journalists dedicated an average of four hours and 57 minutes a week to their favourite books. When asked, most were reading Marquez's *One Hundred Years of Solitude*.

• Taxi drivers (four hours and 46 minutes) preferred biographies (33%), thrillers (24%) and true crime (12%).

• Lawyers (four hours and 33 minutes) were also great crime fans (41%), but they also lapped up gardening, poetry and self-help books.

• Teachers and chefs completed the list (four hours and 27 minutes). They also expressed a preference for Jane Austen and JRR Tolkien.

POETIC PUZZLERS

Who first cried: 'Off with his head'?
Answer on page 145.

LITERARY FEUDS

Many a strong friendship has died at the expense of ideas, and none more so than two of France's most prodigious twentieth-century writers and philosophers. Camus and Sartre met during the German occupation of France in 1943, and quickly became friends. But as the Cold War intensified, East–West relations drew them apart. Sartre believed in violence as a means for change; Camus absolutely did not. They parted as quickly as they met, following a brusque and public quarrel in 1952, after which they never spoke again.

SMOKIE AND THE BROWNIE

Gertrude Stein famously created *The Autobiography of Alice B Toklas* (1933), but the subject, her lifelong companion Alice B Toklas, has also had her own share of literary fame. *The Alice B Toklas Cook Book*, which she put together in 1954, went down in urban legend thanks to one particularly hallucinogenic recipe. Presented as the 'Haschich Fudge, which anyone could whip up on a rainy day', her marijuana-laced brownies were to become the delicacy of choice in many a student kitchen. Here's the recipe, if you want to see what all the fuss was about:

Take one teaspoon black peppercorns, one whole nutmeg, four average sticks of cinnamon, one teaspoon coriander. These should all be pulverised in a mortar. About a handful each of stoned dates, dried figs, shelled almonds and peanuts: chop these and mix them together. A bunch of canibus [sic] sativa can be pulverised. This along with the spices should be dusted over the mixed fruit and nuts, kneaded together. About a cup of sugar dissolved in a big pat of butter. Rolled into a cake and cut into balls about the size of a walnut, it should be eaten with care. Two pieces are quite sufficient.

LIBRARIES WITH A DIFFERENCE

In Kenya, the Camel Library Service brings books to about one million people in isolated villages around the city of Garissa. Since its launch in 1996, the fleet has grown from three to six camels.

The Chilean bookworm Horacio Ogaz travels the outskirts of Chañaral on a tricycle heavily laden with books with his door-to-door library service. However, he's not the only mobile book deliverer in Chile; the 'Book Adventurers' fill their suitcases and backpacks with books to bring the library to the people in Olivar Alto.

In Zimbabwe, remote communities are supplied with services such as book loans, radio, telephone, fax and the internet by 'donkey drawn electrocommunication library carts'.

Floating libraries carry books to people in Alaska, Norway, Sweden and Thailand. Alaska's Kusko Book Express (KBE) reported distributing over 5000 books to more than 1150 students in 2003.

Although there are bookcases in the entrance halls, The Library in Las Vegas isn't a place to visit for books. The kind of learning that goes on here is a more revealing affair: it comes courtesy of librarians who strip rather than shush.

ANAGRAM ANARCHY

Just before the first print run of *Under Milk Wood*, Dylan Thomas altered the name of his Welsh fishing village from Llareggub to Llareggyb. Why the last-minute change? Thomas suddenly realised that, when reversed, the original name spelled 'Buggerall'.

THE WRITTEN WORD

Literary figures who have made their way into the English vernacular...

Bowdlerise – to expurgate a book; from British writer Bowdler (1754–1825), expurgator of Shakespeare

Clerihew – a short comic or nonsensical verse; from British writer Edmund Clerihew Bentley (1875–1956)

Dickensian – poor social conditions; from Charles Dickens

Kafkaesque – an oppressive, nightmarish situation; from Czech author Franz Kafka (1883–1924)

Malapropism – the use of a wrong word for comic effect; from Mrs Malaprop, character in the play *The Rivals* by Irish dramatist Richard Brinsley Sheridan (1751–1816)

Masochism – sexual gratification from one's own pain or humiliation; from Austrian novelist Leopold von Sacher-Masoch (1836–95), who described cases of it

Mentor – an experienced or trusted advisor; from Mentor, Odysseus's loyal friend in Homer's *The Odyssey*

Pander – to gratify or indulge a person, desire or weakness; from Pandarus, a character in poem *Filostrato* by the Italian author Giovanni Boccaccio (1313–1375)

Sadism – sexual gratification from someone else's pain or humiliation; described by the Marquis de Sade (1740–1814)

Svengali – a person who exercises a controlling or mesmerising influence on another; from the character Svengali in *Trilby* by English artist and writer George du Maurier (1834–1896)

Syphilis – venereal disease; from the character Syphilis in the poem *Syphilis seve morbus Gallicus* by Girolamo Fracastro (1483–1553), who was supposed to be the first to suffer from the disease

Wendy House – a small houselike tent; from the house built around Wendy in *Peter Pan* by JM Barrie (1860–1937)

Zany – comically idiotic; from Zanni, the traditional masked clown in the Italian *commedia dell'arte*

FLYING FICTION

The Raven, Edgar Allen Poe
Birdsong, Sebastian Faulks
The Crocodile Bird, Ruth Rendell
Wild Swans, Jung Chang
The Eagle has Landed, Jack Higgins
The Maltese Falcon, Dashiell Hammett
Thorn Birds, Colleen McCullough
To Kill a Mockingbird, Harper Lee
Where Eagles Dare, Alistair MacLean
White Eagles over Serbia, Lawrence Durrell

A LITERARY ROAD TRIP

The world's biggest library is the Library of Congress, Washington DC, USA. It contains 28 million books and has 532 miles of shelving. If you were driving at a constant 70 mph in a car, it would take you just under eight hours to pass them all. The British Library in London is the second largest with 18 million books on its shelves.

TRULY MADLY DEEPLY

Literature's greatest lovers...
Antony and Cleopatra
Heathcliff and Cathy
Odysseus and Penelope
Abelard and Héloise
Tristan and Isolde
Romeo and Juliet
Lady Chatterley and Mellors
Jane Eyre and Mr Rochester
Anna Karenina and Alexei Vronski

THE REWRITE WAS BETTER

Skating for Godot
Trapped in an absurd wait for the arrival of Godot,
Vladimir and Esthergon quarrel, make up, contemplate
suicide, try to sleep, eat a carrot and partake in a spot
of ice-skating.

HOW TO READ

Speed reading isn't just about reading fast (that's 'skimming' apparently). You can actually attend courses that train you to read (and understand) not word-by-word but line-by-line and eventually paragraph-by-paragraph at breakneck speeds. Impatient readers should work their way through the following techniques:

The Hand
Place your right hand sideways on the page and, slowly and evenly, move it straight down the page, following smoothly with your eyes. Gradually increase the speed of your hand to increase the speed of your read.

The Card
Use a card above the line of print to block the words after you've read them. Be sure to push the card down faster than you think you can go and try to read the passage before the words are covered up.

The Sweep
Use your fingers to draw your eyes across the page by sweeping your hand from left to right in a fast, smooth motion under the line that you are reading.

The Hop
Similar to the sweep, except that with the hop you actually lift your fingers and make two even bounces on the line. This method also ensures a steady pace and rhythm.

The Zig-Zag
You know you've arrived when you master the zig-zag. It's the quickest form of scanning and allows you to cut across the text diagonally, picking up words in the whole paragraph rather than each word on a line.

The Skip
The ultimate in speed reading, this unauthorised technique involves jumping from the first to the last page with an optional stop on the middle page for a little more in the way of suspense.

THE BIG BANG

In 2002, gunpowder that may have been used by Guy Fawkes in his attempt to blow up the Houses of Parliament was discovered in the basement of the British Library. It was unearthed in an old stationery box marked with a photograph of the Houses of Parliament (surely a dead giveaway?), which had been given to the library in 1995 as part of the John Evelyn Collection. But both it – and the letter inside in John Evelyn's handwriting suggesting the gunpowder belonged to Guy Fawkes – were revealed only when the collection was being catalogued over seven years later. Talk about sitting on a time bomb.

WHO BORROWED WHAT AND WHEN

Each year Public Lending Right releases data that reveal the most borrowed books and authors in the nation's libraries.

Here are the top picks from July 2002 to June 2003...

1. *The Summons*, John Grisham (2002)
2. *Jinnie*, Josephine Cox (2002)
3. *The Woman Who Left*, Josephine Cox (2001)
4. *Harry Potter and the Chamber of Secrets*, JK Rowling (1999)
5. *Looking Back*, Josephine Cox (2000)
6. *Harry Potter and the Prisoner of Azkaban*, JK Rowling (2000)
7. *Let It Shine*, Josephine Cox (2001)
8. *The Story of Tracy Beaker*, Jacqueline Wilson (1992)
9. *Lizzie Zipmouth*, Jacqueline Wilson (2000)
10. *Girl from the South*, Joanna Trollope (2002)

THE REWRITE WAS BETTER

The Old Man and the Tea
Santiago, an old Cuban fisherman, has the battle of his
life with a ferocious cup of Earl Grey.

LITERARY FESTIVALS

At more than 50 years old, **The Cheltenham Festival of
Literature** (October, www.cheltenhamfestivals.co.uk) is the
longest-running festival of literature in the world. It's also
one of the most comprehensive, with novelists, poets,
dramatists, academics, biographers and even cartoonists
appearing to present their works and answer questions
from the audience. Launched in 1949 by local writer John
Moore, today's event attracts a host of high-profile literary
figures as well as political, showbiz and media personali-
ties, and includes a popular children's festival, Book It!

BURNING ISSUES

If you're not going to do it properly, don't do it all, or so thought Virgil, whose quest for perfection nearly ended in the burning of his 12-book Latin classic *The Aeneid*. The epic, which tells the story of the Trojan prince Aeneas and his wanderings, which led to the foundation of Rome, was 11 years in the writing when the author fell ill returning from a trip to Greece. He had intended to spend another three years editing it into shape and, loathe to let it be published as it stood, demanded on his deathbed that the manuscript be destroyed. Fortunately, the Roman emperor Augustus – who had commissioned the piece – stepped in and arranged for the poem to be published.

Virgil isn't the only author to seek to destroy his written legacy. Franz Kafka also requested that all his work be destroyed just before his death from tuberculosis in 1924.

LITERARY LINGOS

Nadsat (*A Clockwork Orange* – Anthony Burgess, 1962)

A cacophony of Russian and German, of gypsy and cockney slang, and of schoolboy baby talk, Nadsat (the Russian suffix for -teen) is the unintelligible language of Alex de Large and his marauding cohorts. It's a harsh dialect that reflects an even harsher detachment between anti-hero and the 'respectable' society that spawned him. Can you figure it out?

> *We gave this devotchka a tolchock on the litso*
> *and the krovvy came out of her mouth*
> (We gave this girl a blow on the face
> and blood came out of her mouth).

THE SUBTEXT

Subtitles that got lost somewhere along the way...

Black Beauty: The Autobiography of a Horse (Anna
Sewell, 1877)
*Brideshead Revisited: The Sacred and Profane Memories
of Captain Charles Ryder* (Evelyn Waugh, 1945)
The Hunting of the Snark: An Agony in Eight Fits
(Lewis Carroll, 1876)
Fanny Hill: Memoirs of a Woman of Pleasure (John
Cleland, 1748)
Frankenstein, or the Modern Prometheus
(Mary Wollstonecraft Shelley, 1818)
The Hobbit: There and Back Again (JRR Tolkien, 1937)
*Gulliver's Travels, or Travels into Several Remote
Nations of the World* (Jonathan Swift, 1726)
Man and Superman: A Comedy and a Philosophy
(George Bernard Shaw, 1903)
Pamela, or Virtue Rewarded (Samuel Richardson, 1740)
*Slaughterhouse-Five, or Children's Crusade, a Duty
Dance with Death* (Kurt Vonnegut, 1969)
Roots: the Saga of an American Family (Alex Haley, 1976)
*Tess of the D'Urbervilles: A Pure Woman Faithfully
Presented* (Thomas Hardy, 1891)
Twelfth Night, or What You Will (William Shakespeare)
Vanity Fair: A Novel without a Hero (William M
Thackeray, 1847)

LITERARY FEUDS

'Take it on the chin, dear fellow, and move on.'
So spoke VS Naipaul to his friend and protégé Paul
Theroux after Theroux found one of his first editions,
inscribed to Naipaul, listed for sale in a rare-book catalogue
at £1500. The two have argued ever since.

BROUGHT TO BOOK

In 2004, the Canadian portal of Amazon.com accidentally published the real identity of the writers of 'anonymous customer reviews'. Several well-known authors who had promoted their own works and trashed those of their rivals were unmasked. Among them were John Rechy (*City of Night*, 1963) who wrote as 'a reader from Chicago' of the merits of his work *The Life and Adventures of Lyle Clemens* (to which he awarded five stars) and Dave 'a reader from St Louis' Eggers, author of *A Heartbreaking Work of Staggering Genius*, who wrote a gushing review of a work by his friend Heidi Julavits. It's all a far cry from the experiences of Rick Moody, author of *The Ice Storm*, who once wrote of a particularly harsh review posted by his mother on Amazon.com: 'She gave me three out of five stars… and then she told me that it was a positive review.'

PICK UP A PENGUIN

Paperbacks have been around since the seventeenth century, but they really took off with the first 10 Penguins released by Allen Lane in London in 1935. With the motto 'Good books cheap', they cost sixpence a volume – the cheapest a quality book had ever been sold for.

The Penguin symbol was designed by Edward Young in 1935 to mark the spines.

In the early years, colour coding of Penguin covers was used to denote the category of book: orange for fiction; green for crime; light blue for non-fiction; dark blue for biography; cerise for travel; red for theatre; and yellow for miscellany.

The Penguin Pelican imprint was launched in 1937. The books were sold in a Penguincubator, a paperback dispenser, on Charing Cross Road.

In 1956, Lane created Puffins, paperbacks expressly written for children.

PEN PALS

Just to prove the green-eyed monster can be kept at bay, here are some of literature's most famous writing buddies...

Kingsley Amis and Phillip Larkin
Wordsworth and Coleridge
Coleridge remarked that William and Dorothy Wordsworth and himself were 'three persons and one soul'.
TS Eliot and Ezra Pound
Jack Kerouac and Neal Cassady
James Boswell and Samuel Johnson
Franz Kafka and Max Brod
Jack London and Joseph Conrad
Ted Hughes and Seamus Heaney
Henry Miller and Michael Fraenkel
Both made a pact that their correspondence could not end until, together, they had completed one thousand pages of letter writing. Miller may have wanted to see an end to the bet – his final letter was more than 100 pages long.
Ernest Hemingway and F Scott Fitzgerald
Percy Bysshe Shelley and John Keats

THE BIG BOOK

The Bible has 66 books, divided into 1189 chapters consisting of 31,173 verses. Stephen Langton split it into chapters around 1228. R Nathan subsequently divided the Old Testament into verses in 1448, and Ropert Stephanus did likewise for the New Testament in 1551.

The Venerable Bede initiated the first Anglo-Saxon translation of the Bible at the end of the seventh century. By the thirteenth century, Richard Rolle of Hampole began to translate it into Middle English, closely followed by his more famous counterpart, John Wyclif.

Today, the Bible is available in 2233 of the 2700 languages spoken in the world.

LESS IS MORE

A short history of the short story...

Up until the fourteenth century, short stories were mainly used to convey religious morals. With Boccaccio's *The Decameron* and Chaucer's *Canterbury Tales*, the shift moved from the sacred to the profane by focusing on human folly instead.

The English short story changed from verse into prose in the fifteenth century, but it didn't really begin to emerge as a form until the nineteenth century when it took off among American writers, including Nathaniel Hawthorne and Edgar Allan Poe.

In the UK, such writers as Thomas Hardy mastered the genre: his *Wessex Tales* (1888) was the first successful short story by a British author.

Short stories went from strength to strength in the twentieth century, partly because the rise in literary magazines and journals created a market for the genre.

The genre has suffered a bit of a decline in recent years. At least enough for writer Margaret Wilkinson to launch the *Save our Short Story* campaign in 2002. Join the fight and subscribe to the *Endangered Species* online anthology of stories by both known and new writers.

CREATIVE COCK-UPS

In 1889, the editor of the *San Francisco Examiner*, refused to publish the work of Rudyard Kipling with the words: 'I'm sorry Mr Kipling, but you just don't know how to use the English language. This isn't a kindergarten for amateur writers.' Eight years later, Kipling was awarded the Nobel Prize for Literature.

According to Pliny the Elder, Athenian poet **Aeschylus** was killed by a falling tortoise dropped by an eagle in 456 BC.

Italian poet **Dante Alighieri** fell ill and died about an hour after completing *The Divine Comedy* (1321).

Sir Francis Bacon died on 9 April 1626 of suffocation caused by a severe chill, after stuffing a chicken with snow to test his theory of refrigeration.

Lord Byron died in 1824 during a 'blood letting' attempt to cure malarial fever.

William Burroughs accidentally killed his wife when he tried to shoot a glass off her head in Mexico in 1951. He later said that he would never have become a writer but for her death.

British poet **Thomas Chatterton** drank arsenic at the age of 17.

Greek playwright **Euripides** was mauled to death by a pack of wild dogs in 406BC.

William Faulkner died of a heart attack after falling off a horse in 1962.

American poet **Harold Hart Crane** jumped from a steamboat into the Caribbean Sea in 1932.

Ernest Hemingway shot himself in the mouth in Idaho, in 1961.

In 1983, Hungarian-born British author **Arthur Koestler** committed suicide with his wife when he became terminally ill.

American novelist **Jack London** overdosed on morphine in 1916.

In 1593, playwright **Christopher Marlowe**, rumoured to be an Elizabethan secret agent, was stabbed to death in a tavern brawl. He was only 29 years old.

In 1967, English dramatist Joe Orton was killed by his hammer-wielding lover Kenneth Halliwell, who subsequently committed suicide.

Sylvia Plath committed suicide by gassing herself in 1963.

George Bernard Shaw died in 1950, aged 94, after he fell from a ladder while pruning an apple tree.

Percy Bysshe Shelley drowned in a sailing accident off the coast of Italy in 1822.

After giving away his entire fortune, Leo Tolstoy froze to death in a railway station in 1910.

Tennessee Williams choked to death on a bottle cap at his New York City residence on 24 February 1983.

Virginia Woolf committed suicide by drowning herself in the River Ouse near her home in Rodmell, Sussex in 1941.

THE ICE MAN

Since most early literate civilisations were located in warm climes, the first mention of an iceberg in literature didn't occur until the ninth century. It was an Irish traveller, the monk St Brendan, who first recorded the phenomenon of a 'floating mountain of glass' (although he did not know what it was) in *Navigatio Sancti Brendani* ('Voyage of St Brendan'). But Brendan isn't known just for recording the first sight of an ice mountain; faithful followers also believe that the saint discovered the continent of America. He reported a new island far to the west in his writings and, along with the maps of that era, may have given the first indication of its existence to Columbus.

LITERARY LINGOS

Newspeak (*1984* – George Orwell, 1949)
The official language of Oceania, concocted to further the ideological aims of IngSoc (English Socialism) and make all other expression impossible, was widely expected to replace Oldspeak by the middle of the twenty-first century. Riddled with logical contradictions while being grammatically regular, Newspeak was designed to eliminate the possibility of heretical thoughts. The ninth and tenth editions of Orwell's fictitious *Newspeak Dictionary* included such entries as Airstrip One (the new name for an England dominated by the USA), blackwhite (the ability to accept whatever 'truth' the party puts out, no matter how absurd it may be), duckspeak (to speak without thinking) and, of course, Room 101 (the final punishment for 'thoughtcriminals' in the Ministry of Love).

READ WITH MOTHER

The nation's favourite children's poems according to a 2001 BBC poll...

1. *The Owl and the Pussy Cat* – Edward Lear
2. *Matilda* – Hilaire Belloc
3. *Don't* – Michael Rosen
4. *Jabberwocky* – Lewis Carroll
5. *On the Ning Nang Nong* – Spike Milligan
6. *Talking Turkeys!!* – Benjamin Zephaniah
7. *Macavity the Mystery Cat* – TS Eliot
8. *The King's Breakfast* – AA Milne
9. *Please Mrs Butler* – Allan Ahlberg
10. *Down with Children! Do Them In!* – Roald Dahl

WHEN TO JUDGE A BOOK BY ITS COVER

Over the years, books have been bound in some of the most fitting of materials:

Asbestos – *Fahrenheit 451* (Ray Bradbury, 1953)
Black lace panties – *Grand Opening: A Year in the Life of a Total Wife* (Alice Whitman Leeds, 1980)
Cigar box – *The Soverane Herbe: A History of Tobacco* (WA Penn, 1901)
Cricket blazer – *Baxter's Second Innings* (Henry Drummond, 1892)
Fish skin – *The Compleat Angler* (Izaak Walton, 1653)
Handkerchief – *The Love Sonnets of a Hoodlum* (Wallace Irwin, 1901)
Human skin – *Poetical Works* (John Milton, 1645)
Bound in the skin of a murderer, Milton's wasn't the only work to befit such a cover. During the French Revolution, a copy of the new constitution was bound with the tanned leather skin of a guillotined aristocrat.
Japanese Silk – *Quicksilver* (Neal Stephenson, 2003)
Skunk skin – *Mein Kampf* (Adolf Hitler, 1925)
Plywood – *Modern Plywood* (Thomas D Perry, 1942)
Sheets – *The Rise and Fall of Carol Banks* (Elliott W Springs, 1931)
Soldier's uniform – *All Quiet on the Western Front* (Erich Maria Remarque, 1929)

EASY, MY FRIEND WATSON

It's one of the world's most famous catchphrases, but in reality, Sherlock Holmes never once uttered, 'Elementary, my dear Watson' – not in the books that is. The oft-quoted phrase, like Holmes' curved calabash pipe (introduced by actor William Gillette) and deerstalker hat, was a creation of the film adaptation.

WHAT'S WHAT IN A BOOK

The printer begins with a large sheet; if the sheet is folded once so as to form two 'leaves' of four pages, the book is a **folio** (Latin for leaf); a sheet folded twice into four 'leaves' is a **quarto**; a sheet folded three times into eight leaves is an **octavo** (the most frequently used size in modern printing). In a **duodecimo** volume, a sheet is folded to make 12 leaves.

As the book is open in front of you, the page on the right is called a **recto,** and the page on the left a **verso.**

The **colophon** in older books was a note at the end stating such facts as the title, author, printer and date of issue. In modern books the colophon is ordinarily in the front, on the title page.

Incunabula (pl. incunables), the term given to books printed before 1500, derives from the Latin for 'swaddling clothes'. It describes the 'infancy' of books published before the invention of the Gutenberg Press.

The word 'edition' now designates the total copies of a book that are printed from the same setting of type. A **variorum** edition designates either an edition of work that lists all the textual variants in an author's manuscripts and printed revisions, or an edition that includes a selection of annotations and commentaries on the text by earlier editors and critics.

POETIC PUZZLERS

In John Fowles' novel, who is the French lieutenant's woman?
Answer on page 145.

I <u>WILL</u> GO TO THE BALL

A favourite fairytale character of young girls all over the world, Cinderella has appeared in a variety of guises...

• In China, she's known as Yeh-Shen; in the Algonquin Indians of North America as the Rough-Face Girl; and in parts of Africa as Chinye and Nyasha. Scholars disagree about the exact number of variations that exist, but it is estimated to be somewhere between 340 and 3000.

• The earliest known version originated in China. Recorded by Tuan Ch'engshih in the middle of the ninth century, it centres around the beautiful Yeh-Shen, who is relegated to the function of maid after her father remarries. In this cautionary tale, the stepmother and evil stepsister are stoned to death for their cruelty.

• The British put a slight twist on the story in *Tattercoats*. This moral parable has the evil stepmother replaced by a loveless grandfather.

• The Grimm brothers retold an even less forgiving version with *Aschenputtel* ('Ash Girl'). In the Grimm version, the stepsisters are left permanently blinded after their eyes have been pecked out by birds.

• In 1697, French author Charles Perrault published *Contes de ma Mere l'Oye* ('Tales of Mother Goose'). It included the Cinderella story that was later immortalised by Walt Disney. However, in Perrault's original tale, Cinderella's slippers were made out of fur. The story was changed in the 1600s by a translator who confused vair, French for 'fur', with verre, French for 'glass'.

THE REWRITE WAS BETTER

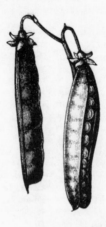

War and Peas
An epic study of the Napoleonic war and
a celebration of the small vegetable that resolved it.

POETIC PUZZLERS

My first is in poetry, but never in song
My second's in Ireland, where I do come from
My third is in heat, but never in cold
My fourth is in centre, that which cannot hold
My fifth is in second, and also in still
My whole is a poet whose first name is Bill
Answer on page 145.

CREATIVE COCK-UPS

Experimental writer Gertrude Stein has had her share of mockery for her loose and rambling writing style, and no more so than from her editor, AJ Fifield, who sent her the following rejection: 'I am only one, only one, only one. Only one being, one at the same time. Not two, not three, only one. Only one life to live, only 60 minutes in one hour. Only one pair of eyes. Only one brain. Only one being. Being only one, having only one pair of eyes, having only one time, having only one life, I cannot read your MS three or four times. Not even one time. Only one look, only one look is enough. Hardly one copy would sell here. Hardly one. Hardly one.'

THE WORST WITCH

The magical tale of an orphaned boy who discovers his wizard heritage at an unusual boarding school for magicians has won the hearts of millions, and the suspicions of a few. Pottermania, it seems, has a dark side.

At its strongest in the USA, a growing movement is targeting the seven-book series for the propagation of the word of the devil. They contend that the books are merely Satan's cover in his ultimate plan to plant immorality and corruption in the minds of the nation's children. Christian societies are becoming passionately divided on the issue, schools are banning them on the grounds that they are sacreligious and entire families are refusing to buy them because the occult skills they allegedly contain (witchcraft, sorcery, casting spells, spiritualism, interpreting omens and 'calling up the dead') are considered 'an abomination to the Lord'.

It appears that the UK's most beloved young hero isn't quite as humble and courageous as was once thought.

WHAT'S IN A NAME?

A good title, they say, is the title of a successful book, but it's not always easy to get there. Here are some working titles that didn't make the cut. The question is: would the novels still have hit the big time if the titles hadn't been changed?

A Portrait of the Artist as a Young Man (James Joyce, 1916)
Working Title: 'Stephen Hero'

Catch-22 (Joseph Heller, 1961)
Working Title: 'Catch-18'

David Copperfield (Charles Dickens, 1849)
Working Title: 'Mag's Diversions'

The Great Gatsby (F Scott Fitzgerald, 1925)
Working Title: 'Incident at West Egg'. Fitzgerald also suggested 'The High-Bouncing Lover' and 'Under the Red White and Blue', which his editor fortunately chose to ignore.

Gone with the Wind (Margaret Mitchell, 1936)
Working Title: 'Ba! Ba! Black Sheep'

Lady Chatterley's Lover (DH Lawrence, 1928)
Working Title: 'John Thomas and Lady Jane'. Lawrence once mused that, but for its racy title, the book would not have been banned. Surely his proposed euphemisms wouldn't have fared much better.

Pride and Prejudice (Jane Austen, 1831)
Working Title: 'First Impressions'

Treasure Island (Robert Louis Stevenson, 1883)
Working Title: 'The Sea-Cook'

War and Peace (Leo Tolstoy, 1866)
Working Title: 'All's Well that Ends Well'.

The Wasteland (TS Eliot, 1922)
Working Title: 'He do the Police in Different Voices'. It's a quote from Charles Dickens' *Our Mutual Friend*.

PSEUDONYMS FOR LIFE

Authors who first created their names and then penned their works...

Voltaire – Francois-Marie Arouet

Stendhal – Marie-Henri Beyle

Anthony Burgess – John Wilson

Lewis Carroll – Charles Lutwidge Dodgson
Dodgson created his pen name by transposing
and Latinizing his first two names.

Molière – Jean Baptiste Poquelin

George Orwell – Eric Arthur Blair

Dr Seuss – Theodore Seuss Geisel

Mark Twain – Samuel Langhorn Clemens

John le Carré – David Cornwell

Katherine Mansfield – Katherine Beauchamp

Daniel Defoe – Daniel Foe

Jack London – John Griffith

Enid Blyton – Mrs Daryl Walters

TONGUE TWISTERS

The longest word in the English language, according
to the Oxford English Dictionary, is
pneumonoultramicroscopicsilicovolcanoconiosis.

The only other word with the same amount of letters is
pneumonoultramicroscopicsilicovolcanoconioses,
the plural form.

BOOKS IN HIGH PLACES

Just to prove running the country isn't a full-time job, four-time Prime Minister William Ewart Gladstone also managed to devise in his free time a storage system now in use in the Bodleian Library in Oxford. *On Books and the Housing of Them* (1898), a brief 29-page study of the looming problems of book shelving at the major libraries of the time, even went right down to studies of the spacing of shelves, what size lumber to use and how to organise your collection. As if that isn't enough, Gladstone also offers recommendations on the proper of style of binding to match the book and which books should never share the same shelf; such as Conservative and Labour manifestos, perhaps.

LITERARY FEUDS

It seems even Vladimir Nabokov, the quintessential European intellectual aristocrat, couldn't escape the pettiness of minor quibbling. His friendship with his former mentor, the influential literary critic and young editor of *The New Republic* Edmund Wilson, fell foul of a dose of creative criticism. Nabokov asked for his friend's 'honest' opinion on the pre-release copy of *Lolita* (and we all know what that really means), to which Wilson replied: 'I like it less than anything else of yours I have read' and called the characters and situations 'repulsive' and 'unreal'. Nabokov's nymphet made history, but so did their feud – they argued to their deathbeds.

LITERARY BANDWAGONS

The Lost Generation

Named by Gertrude Stein and led (in public perception at least) by Ernest Hemingway, the young writers who sailed from the USA for Paris shortly after World War One – beset with post-war disillusionment and the first clawings of twentieth-century ennui – left in search of creative fulfilment and the bohemian lifestyle. And, for the most part, they found it. Drinking, writing and copulating their way around Paris, Hemingway, John Dos Passos, F Scott Fitzgerald and Henry Miller (to name the brightest stars among many) challenged literary convention with mixed success. Not that 'success' was ever really the issue, as Miller declares in *Tropic of Cancer*: 'I am not interested in perfecting my thoughts nor my action… It is the triumph of the individual over art.'

WHERE CAN YOU FIND A FILING CABINET IN THE WONDERFUL WIZARD OF OZ?

Legend has it that L Frank Baum's make-believe land took its name from a cabinet drawer labelled O–Z, which was situated in front of him while he was putting his tale to paper. He corroborated the story in a press release for the book in 1903: 'I have a little cabinet letter file on my desk that is just in front of me. I was thinking and wondering about a title for the story, and had settled on the "Wizard" as part of it. My gaze was caught by the gilt letters on the three drawers of the cabinet. The first was A–G; the next drawer was labeled H–N; and on the last were the letters O–Z. And "Oz" it at once became.'

THE REWRITE WAS BETTER

Vanity Chair
The ruthless Becky Sharp defies her impoverished
background to clamber up the class ladder and nab
herself an elegant chaise longue.

THE POWER AND THE GLORY

When *Book Club News* ran a competition offering a prize
for the best parody of Graham Greene's work in 1949,
the entries came in thick and fast. After selecting and publishing a winner, the magazine was surprised to receive
a letter from the author himself: 'While I was overjoyed
that Mr John Smith had won the contest,' Greene wrote,
'I felt that John Doakes and William Jones were also
deserving of prizes.' Greene had sent in all three entries –
they were rejected passages from earlier works.

LIBRARY FINES

Library fines vary from city to city and from borough to borough, but here's roughly what you can expect to pay...

Ten pence per day per item for the first week the item is overdue
Forty pence per week after the first week
Maximum fine: **£10 per item**

Exemptions from fines apply to senior citizens (60 years and over), children and young adults (18 years and younger), members on state benefits (Jobseekers Allowance or income support) and users of the Mobile Library.

If you don't have the time to drop off the books, you can always renew your books over the phone. Books can be renewed up to three times without bringing them back to the library, unless they have been reserved by another borrower.

A TALE OF TWO INMATES

Marco Polo (1254–1324), author of one of the Western world's most famous travelogues, may not even have written it down on paper if he hadn't been captured by the Genoese and imprisoned for a year. Three years after Marco returned to Venice from his historic 24-year adventure in the Far and Middle East, he was captured during fighting with the rival city of Genova, where he found himself holed up with a writer of romances named Rustichello di Pisa.

It was only when prompted by Rustichello that Marco Polo dictated the story of his travels, which, published as *The Description of the World or The Travels of Marco Polo*, became one of the most popular books in medieval Europe.

POETIC CRIB

Blank Verse
A verse with no rhyme but plenty of meter. The form tends to favour ten-syllable iambic pentameters as used by Shakespeare in his dramas and by Milton in Paradise Lost.

Clerihew
A pair of couplets that rhyme AABB and usually describe a person.

Concrete poetry
Free-form verse, relying heavily upon its visual impact on the printed page.

Limerick
A five-line jingle rhymed AABBA.

Haiku
A Japanese lyric of 17 syllables split into three lines of five, seven and five syllables.

Heroic couplets
A two-line couplet in iambic pentameter often used in epic and narrative poetry.

Epic
A continuous narrative poem, celebrating a hero or an event.

Ode
A poem, originally intended to be sung, addressed to someone or something.

Sonnet
A poem of 14 lines. A Shakespearean sonnet splits the 14 lines into three groups of four and follows them with a couplet (rhyming ABAB CDCD EFEF GG); a Miltonic sonnet splits the 14 lines into two groups of eight and six (rhyming ABBAABBA CDECDE).

CARRY AND CASH

If you've ever wondered whether an author gets paid for the reading of books borrowed from public libraries, then the answer is yes. The Public Lending Right Act came into being in 1979 after years of writers complaining that they didn't receive a penny in profit no matter how many times their books were borrowed from a library. The act entitled the author to a payment – currently just over four pence per book up to a maximum of £6000 – per issue. To make it easier to enforce, royalties are based on a carefully monitored sample of libraries throughout Britain.

LITERARY LINGOS

Tlön, Uqbar and Tertius Orbis
(*Labyrinths* – Jorge Luis Borges, 1964)

A single mention in an out-of-print edition of the *Encyclopedia Britannica* is all Borges initially had to fuel his interest in the planet Tlön and its mysterious languages – some that are without verbs, others without nouns. As years pass, however, and chance experience repeatedly throws up interesting titbits about this planet so profoundly different from Earth, he still comes no closer to establishing whether Tlön, and it's languages like Tertius Orbis, ever actually existed or whether they are just the elaborate construct of a renegade intellectual clique.

POETIC PUZZLERS

In the DH Lawrence novel, who was
Lady Chatterley's lover?
Answer on page 145.

Victor Hugo was a madman who thought he was Victor Hugo. *Jean Cocteau*

The high-water mark, so to speak, of Socialist literature is WH Auden, a sort of gutless Kipling. *George Orwell*

I was reading Proust for the first time. Very poor stuff. I think he was mentally defective. *Evelyn Waugh*

Kingsley Amis once said that sex is a great cure for a hangover, which, indeed must be the case, because if you thought Kingsley Amis was going to make love to you, you'd certainly avoid getting drunk in the first place. *Joseph O'Connor*

Mr Wordsworth never ruined anyone's morals, unless, perhaps, he has driven some susceptible persons to a crime in the very fury of boredom. *Ezra Pound*

A demagogic Welsh masturbator who failed to pay his bills. *Robert Graves on Dylan Thomas*

There are two ways of disliking poetry. One way is to dislike it; the other is to read Pope. *Oscar Wilde*

If you imagine a Scotch commercial traveller in a Scotch commercial hotel leaning on the bar and calling the barmaid Dearie, then you will know the keynote of Burns' verse. *AE Housman*

Joseph Heller's *God Knows* even looks exactly like a real book, with pages and print and dust jacket and everything. This disguise is extremely clever, considering the contents; the longest lounge act never performed in the history of the Catskills. *Paul Gray*

HG Wells throws information at the reader as if emptying his mind like a perpetual chamber pot from a window. *Henry James*

Mr C had talent, but he couldn't spel. No man had a right to be a lit'rary man onless he knows how to spel. It is a pity that Chawcer, who had geneyus, was so unedicated. He's the wus speller I know of.
Artumus Ward

It is the most insipid ridiculous play that ever I saw in my life.
Samuel Pepys, in his Diary

(29 September 1662) after viewing A Midsummer's Night Dream

With the single exception of Homer, there is no eminent writer, not even Sir Walter Scott, whom I can despise so entirely as Shakespear.
George Bernard Shaw (who always insisted on spelling Shakespeare without the final 'e').

TOP TEN EUPHEMISMS
FOR ROMANCE FANS

10. Her heaving breasts

9. His punishing kiss

8. Her liquid centre

7. His rigid member

6. Her sensitive bud

5. His stirring loin

4. Her nubbin of flesh

3. His throbbing manhood

2. Her bucking hips

1. His growl of release

MAN'S MACHINES

Good or evil, robots have appeared in literature since Homer first wrote of maidens made of gold and the bronze giant Talos in *The Iliad*; here are our top-ten robotic creations...

- The robotic chess-player in Ambrose Bierce's *Moxon's Master* (1894)
- The evil Cyclops intent on zapping the world in HG Well's *The War of the Worlds* (1898)
- The tin woodsman in L Frank Baum's Oz books (1900) – 'If I only had a heart...'
- The Martian robot in John Wyndham's *The Lost Machine* (1932)
- The robotic surgeon in Harl Vincent's *Rex* (1934)
- The robots who discover their roots in Robert Moore Williams' *Robots Return* (1938)
- *The Iron Man*, in the book of the same name by Ted Hughes (1968)
- The perfect-looking, obedient robot replicas conceived to replace women in Ira Levin's *The Stepford Wives* (1972)
- Andrew Martin from *The Bicentennial Man* (1976)
- The fully organic androids produced by genetic engineering in Philip K Dick's *Do Androids Dream of Electric Sheep?* (1968)

LITERARY LINGOS

Nerd – Coined by Dr Seuss in *If I Ran the Zoo* (1950)

Robot – First appeared in Czech playwright Karl Capek's *RUR* (1920), as a derivation of the Czech word for work (robota)

Heavy metal – Penned by William Burroughs in *The Naked Lunch* (1959)

LITERARY LOVE

Romances that blossomed over a book launch or two...

*Margaret Drabble
and Michael Holroyd*
Novelist Margaret Drabble and biographer Michael Holroyd have been husband and wife since the early 1980s.

*Sylvia Plath
and Ted Hughes*
One of the best known literary matches, famous for its tumultuous and destructive edge.

Rimbaud and Verlaine
Two French poets who embarked on a passionate relationship fuelled by absinthe and hashish. After Rimbaud threatened to finish it in 1873, Verlaine shot him and was imprisoned for two years.

*Virginia Woolf
and Vita Sackville-West*
A love affair that provided Woolf with the inspiration for *Orlando*.

*Lord Byron
and Lady Caroline Lamb*
Novelist Lamb is best known for her short but tempestuous relationship with poet Byron. He ended the affair after four months; she termed him 'mad, bad and dangerous to know'.

*Simone de Beauvoir
and Jean-Paul Sartre*
These two influential philosophers and novelists, who were among the first proponents of existentialism, socialism and anti-colonialism, really were a match made in heaven.

*Claire Tomalin
and Michael Frayn*
Biographer and editor Claire Tomalin meets playwright and novelist Michael Frayn, both independent winners of the Whitbread Novel Award. Love, prizes, success follows... What more do you need?

BOOK SENSATIONS

Hundreds of meaningless words litter our lives, but what about those common experiences, feelings and situations, which no word can adequately describe? In *The Meaning of Liff* and *The Deeper Meaning of Liff*, Douglas Adams and John Lloyd solve the problem by ambushing the names of our towns and reapplying them where they are needed most. Here are their thoughts on all things literary...

Ahenny (*adj.*) – the way people stand when examining other people's bookshelves.

Ainderby Quernhow (*n.*) – One who continually bemoans the 'loss' of the word 'gay' to the English language, even though they had never used the word in any context at all until they started complaining they couldn't use it anymore.

Bathel (*vb.*) – to pretend to have read the book under discussion when in fact you've only seen the TV series.

Beppy (*n.*) – the triumphal slamming shut of a book after reading the final page.

Dalmilling (*ptcpl.vb.*) – continually making small talk to someone who is trying to read a book.

Fritham (*n.*) – a paragraph that gets you stuck in a book. The more you read it, the less it means to you.

Great Wakering (*ptcpl.vb.*) – the panic which sets in when you badly need to go to the lavatory and cannot make up your mind about what book or magazine to take with you.

Great Tosson (*n.*) – a fat book containing four words and six cartoons which costs £12.95.

Liff (*n.*) – a book, the contents of which are totally belied by its cover. For instance, any book the dust jacket of which bears the words, 'This book will change your life'.

Pulverbatch (*n.*) – the first paragraph on the blurb of a dust-jacket in which famous authors claim to have had a series of menial jobs in their youth.

Ripon (*vb.*) – to include all the best jokes from the book in a review to make it look as if the critic thought of them.

POETIC PUZZLERS

Which of his novels did Charles Dickens say
he liked the best?
Answer on page 145.

BRITAIN'S TOP PUBLIC INTELLECTUALS

When British monthly, *Prospect* magazine, asked:
'Who are Britain's top 100 public intellectuals?' in 2004,
the following literary types made the list:

Martin Amis (novelist and critic)
Melvyn Bragg (broadcaster and writer)
AS Byatt (critic and writer)
John Carey (literature professor and critic)
Matthew D'Ancona (journalist and writer)
Terry Eagleton (literary theorist)
Michael Frayn (playwright and novelist)
AC Grayling (philosopher, writer and journalist)
Germaine Greer (writer and feminist)
David Hare (playwright)
Seamus Heaney (poet)
Frank Kermode (literary critic and writer)
Ian McEwan (novelist)
VS Naipaul (novelist and essayist)
Melanie Phillips (author and columnist)
Philip Pullman (children's author)
Salman Rushdie (writer)
Roger Scruton (philosopher and writer)
Gitta Sereny (biographer)
George Steiner (writer and academic)
Tom Stoppard (playwright)
Jeanette Winterson (novelist)
James Wood (literary critic)

The Cat is the Hat

LITERARY FEUDS

Influential philosopher Jean-Jacques Rousseau launched a career by advocating the 'innate goodness of humans', but it seems he didn't always believe what he preached. When David Hume, Scotland's prized philosopher, invited Rousseau to England in 1766, the French intellectual became increasingly convinced that Hume, his friend and benefactor, and the British government's spies were set on killing him. After a year in his paranoid company, Hume understandably retracted his earlier assertion that 'there is no man in Europe of whom I have entertained a higher idea'.

TOP TEN FICTIONAL PARTNERSHIPS

Every Batman needs his Robin...

Hansel and Gretel
Jim Casy and Tom Joad (*The Grapes of Wrath*)
Dante and Virgil (*The Divine Comedy*)
Jeeves and Wooster
Winston Smith and Julia (*1984*)
Lenny and George (*Of Mice and Men*)
Jekyll and Hyde
Frodo Baggins and Samwise Gamgee
(*The Lord of the Rings*)
Sherlock Holmes and Dr Watson
Vladimir and Estragon (*Waiting for Godot*)

LITERARY BANDWAGONS

The Bloomsbury Group

During the years between 1904 and World War Two, a number of Cambridge graduates would meet with their closest friends for drinks and conversation in Bloomsbury. This informal gathering subsequently became known as an immensely creative, productive and influential meeting of minds. With Virginia Woolf, EM Forster, Lytton Strachey and John Meynard Keynes among its members, the Bloomsbury group was committed to a rejection of Victorian values on all fronts – moral, artistic and sexual. Resented by some as a snobbish clique, The Bloomsbury group has since become just as famous for the romantic entanglements of several of its members as it has for their individual creative achievements.

AN ENCYCLOPEDIC HISTORY

The term 'encyclopedia' comes from the Greek *enkyklios paideia*, which translates as 'a circle of learning'.

The first attempt at an encyclopedia was made more than 2000 years ago, but the name encyclopedia was not used for such works until the sixteenth century.

Greek philosopher Aristotle is known as the 'father of encyclopedias' because of his written attempts to summarise all existing knowledge. But the first encyclopedia is said to have been compiled in the fourth century BC by Greek philosopher Speusippus, a student of Plato.

Natural History (c. 77 AD) by the Roman scholar Pliny the Elder is the oldest complete encyclopedia still in existence. It has 37 volumes and remained popular for almost 1500 years.

Etymologies, or Origins (623 AD) was compiled by Spanish scholar Saint Isidore of Seville and included subjects such as medicine, animals, the earth, grammar, war and games.

The largest encyclopedia was created in the sixteenth century by the Chinese. The *Yung Lo Ta Tien* was compiled by over 5000 writers and bound in more than 11,000 volumes.

Encyclopedias were for centuries arranged so that they began with God and angels. English philosopher and statesman Francis Bacon was the first to organise a proper structure for his *The Great Reconstruction* (1620), but it was never completed.

The alphabetical and subject arrangement of encyclopedias began in the eighteenth century. French philosopher and critic Pierre Bayle's two-volume *Historical and Critical Dictionary* (1697) was famed for its simplicity and clarity.

The 28-volume *Encyclopédie* (1751–1772) compiled by French philosopher and dramatist Denis Diderot employed a team of mathematicians, philosophers and academics and claimed 'to exhibit as far as possible the order and system of human knowledge, and contain the fundamental principles and essential details of every science and art, whether liberal or mechanical'.

Encyclopedia Britannica was first published in 100 parts from 1768 to 1771 before being bound into three volumes.

The first CD-ROM encyclopedia was produced in 1985, and in 1993 Microsoft released *Encarta Encyclopedia*, the first to have no accompanying books.

POOP FICTION

Warning: these books may cause flatulence...

'Walter the Farting Dog' is a flatulent pooch whose little problem saves the day in the series of books by William Kotzwinkle and Glenn Murray, which begins: 'Gas. He can't help it. It's just the way he is.'

In *The Adventures of Captain Underpants* our Y-fronted hero fights for truth, justice and all that is cotton with the motto: 'Never underestimate the power of underwear'. The brainchild of Dav Pilkey, the stories see his superhero attempting such dangerous challenges as leaping tall buildings without getting a wedgie and doing battle with the evil Professor Poopypants.

Andy Griffiths' *The Day my Butt Went Psycho* follows a 12-year-old named Zack, whose backside is prone to detaching itself and making trouble. He followed it up with *Zombie Butts from Uranus*, in which Zack is again on hand to rid the earth of the stinky space invaders.

CREATIVE COCK-UPS

When *The Lord of the Rings* was published in 1950, JRR Tolkien, then professor of ancient languages at Oxford, may have been slightly surprised to learn that it would eventually sell more than 100 million copies. But he was certainly surprised by the cover illustration used for the first American paperback edition. 'I think the cover ugly,' he wrote to his publisher at Ballantine, 'but I recognise that a main object of a paperback cover is to attract purchases, and I suppose that you are better judges of what is attractive in the USA than I am. I therefore will not enter into a debate about taste, but I must ask this about the vignette: What has it got to do with the story? Where is this place? Why a lion and emus? And what is the thing in the foreground with pink bulbs? I do not understand how anybody who had read the tale (I hope you are one) could think such a picture would please the author.'

When Tolkien later confronted his publisher, he found his concerns to be justified – neither the illustrator nor the publisher had 'had time' to read the work.

NAME DROPPERS

First names of writers better known by other names

Lord Byron – George
Colette – Sidonie
Harper Lee – Nelle
Ogden Nash – Frederic
Beatrix Potter – Helen
Rudyard Kipling – Joseph
Salman Rushdie – Ahmed
Virginia Woolf – Adeline

LITERARY PRIZES

The Nobel Prize for Literature takes its name and foundation from Alfred Nobel, brilliant scientist, literary intellectual and philanthropist, who left instructions for the prize categories (chemistry, physics, medicine, literature, peace, economics) in his will.

The first winner was Sully Prud'Homme, the French Poet Laureate, in 1901.

The first British winner was Rudyard Kipling in 1907. He was also the youngest to pick up the prize, receiving it at the age of 42.

The last British nominee to receive the prize was Winston Churchill – he picked it up in 1953 at the age of 79.

The oldest winner was also British. Bertrand Russell accepted the prize in 1950 when he was 78.

William Faulkner's Nobel Prize was awarded a year late – in 1950 – because the committee couldn't make up its mind in time. It was reportedly one of the most difficult decisions in the award's history, as the list also included Hemingway, Steinbeck, Pasternak, Sholokhov, Mauriac, Camus and Winston Churchill.

The only winner to have declined the prize was Jean-Paul Sartre. He refused it in 1964, apparently because he believed Pablo Neruda should have won it.

The first American woman to pick up the award was Pearl Buck. She received it in 1938 at the age of 46.

POETIC PUZZLERS

In the Shakespeare play, who was the merchant of Venice?
Answer on page 146.

POETIC CRIB

Simile – comparison between two distinctly different things marked by 'like' or 'as': 'my love is like a red, red rose' (Robert Burns)

Metaphor – application of a distinctly different type of thing without asserting a comparison: 'My love is a red, red rose'

Mixed metaphor – combination of two diverse metaphoric vehicles: 'To take arms against a sea of trouble/ And by opposing end them' (Shakespeare, *Hamlet*)

Dead metaphor – metaphors so overused that we are no longer aware of the difference: 'leg of a table', 'heart of the matter'

Metonymy (Greek for a change of name) – application of one common term for another: the 'Crown' (for the Monarch)

Synecdoche (Greek for taking together) – using a part of something to signify a whole: a 'hundred sails' (for ships)

A BARDLESS WORLD

Unimaginable it may seem, but we could now have a world without Shakespeare. The Bard's genius was little appreciated during his lifetime and as the years passed, his work was first criticised and then forgotten. Seven years after his death in 1616, two actors in his company, John Heminge and Henry Condell, resurrected the original copies and scratched together the funds to publish them in one authoritative volume: the first folio. History has proved their enthusiasm justified, even though it wasn't until 1769, after the first Stratford Festival, that 'Bardolatry' really took off.

MURDER SHE WROTE

When police found the car of 36-year-old Agatha Christie hidden in a clump of bushes a dozen or so miles away from her Berkshire home, on the morning of the 4 December 1926, they suspected first suicide and then murder. But while it seemed that prime suspect Archibald Christie, Agatha's husband, might stand to gain from the death of his wife, he had a pretty solid alibi for the night of her disappearance. Where was he? At a weekend party in Surrey with his mistress, Nancy Neele.

Just 11 days after the author disappeared, a waiter revealed her whereabouts – she had been hiding out in a hotel in Harrogate, Yorkshire, under the assumed name of Teresa Neele. Archibald originally claimed that his wife had lost her memory (no one believed his story, least of all the Surrey police who presented him with a bill for the cost of the search) and it wasn't until after the detective writer's death that the truth finally emerged.

It seems the author had found out about his affair and concocted the plan to scare her husband into leaving his mistress. It didn't work – they were divorced two years later.

MUFFIN MATTERS

There's a champion on hand for all those book readers who have spent their literary lives chastised for creasing the book spine, folding over the corners or dropping crumbs on their newest read. Charles Lamb is one of many who believed that a book kept in pristine condition couldn't match one we've left our fingerprints on. 'A book reads the better,' he wrote, 'which is our own, and has been so long known to us, that we know the topography of its blots, and dog's ears, and we can trace the dirt in it to having read it at tea with buttered muffins.'

TOP TEN LITERARY VILLAINS

Good has been pitted against evil since the earliest literary texts; here are some of the best bad boys (and machines)…

Big Brother – The all-seeing dictator of Oceania in George Orwell's *1984*

Captain Ahab – The deranged captain intent on killing the white whale in Herman Melville's *Moby-Dick*

Captain Hook – Peter Pan's hooked nemesis from JM Barrie's *Peter Pan and Wendy*

Grendel – The monstrous demon from the old English epic *Beowulf*

Iago – The treacherous backstabber in Shakespeare's *Othello*

Jack – William Golding's cruel and power-hungry youth leader in *The Lord of the Flies*

Mr Kurtz – The tortured villain of Joseph Conrad's novel *Heart of Darkness*

Satan – The ruler of hell in John Milton's **Paradise Lost** and Dante's **The Divine Comedy**

Sauron – The dark lord in JRR Tolkien's *The Lord of the Rings*

Scrooge, Ebenezer – The villain turned hero in Charles Dickens' *A Christmas Carol*

BOOK RECORDS

The record for unsupported book balancing goes to John Evans of Sheffield. In 1998, he balanced no fewer than 62 identical books on his head – that's a book tower 185.4cm (73in) in height.

Before fame, many a writer has been forced into the odd period of nine-to-five; here are some before-they-were-famous occupations, some of them little known...

Joseph Conrad was a merchant sailor for 20 years.

Salman Rushdie spent many a year working in advertising. He thought up the cream cakes strap line 'Naughty but nice'.

Sylvia Plath worked as a receptionist at a psychiatric clinic.

John Milton was appointed Secretary for the Foreign Tongues.

In 1970, **Hunter S Thompson** stood for election of Sheriff of Pitkin, Colorado, with a 'freak power' campaign. He lost by a handful of votes.

Thomas Hardy trained as an architect.

While broadcasting wartime propaganda for the BBC during World War Two, **Orwell** worked in an office numbered 101. He also served as a British Civil Servant in India for and as an officer of the Indian Imperial Police.

Lewis Carroll was deacon and maths teacher at Oxford.

Edgar Allan Poe spent a number of years editing and writing for magazines and newspapers. Unfortunately, his inability to hold his liquor got him fired from each job.

Kingsley Amis supplemented his income as a university lecturer.

Charles Dickens first worked as a court stenographer and a shoe factory worker.

TS Eliot was rather boringly a clerk at Lloyds Bank.

JRR Tolkien was professor of English at Oxford University.

THE REWRITE WAS BETTER

Oliver Pissed
Born into a workhouse in 1830s England, a difficult life
of crime and grime leaves its mark on Oliver Pissed.

WHEN MIDDLE BECAME MODERN

Sometime during the fifteenth or sixteenth centuries,
Middle English became modern English with the dramatic
change in vowel pronunciations that has since become
known as the 'Great Vowel Shift'. The Middle English long
'i' (formerly pronounced like the modern 'e') shifted to the
current 'i' as in high, the Middle English 'sheep' (formerly
pronounced 'shape') changed to the modern 'sheep' and the
Middle English 'hous' (pronounced 'hoose') to the modern
'house' in a general movement forward of 'long' vowel
sounds in the mouth.

The change happened so fast that only 50 years after
Geoffrey Chaucer wrote *The Canterbury Tales*, his readers
were pronouncing his words in completely different ways.

PERFECT WORLDS

Sir Thomas More first coined the term 'utopia' (a pun meaning both 'good land' and 'nowhere land' in Greek) for his 1515 work. Generations of authors have since offered their own fantastic takes on both utopia and dystopia...

1984 – George Orwell

The Book of the New Moral World – Robert Owen
Owen founded the community of New Harmony, Indiana, but it failed in 1831, as did most of his experiments in utopian socialism.

Brave New World – Aldous Huxley

Gormenghast – Mervyn Peake

Gulliver's Travels – Jonathan Swift
The island of the Houyhnhnms is proffered as the world's most perfect society, as opposed to the manlike yahoos.

Lost Horizon – James Hilton
It marked the first use of the term 'Shangri-la' to describe a hidden paradise

Riddley Walker – Russell Hoban

The Time Machine – HG Wells

Walden Two – BF Skinner
Skinner believed that humans are a product of their conditioning, so children in his Utopia are raised and educated in a manner that many critics have compared to brainwashing.

POETIC PUZZLERS

In Oliver Goldsmith's 1766 novel, who was the vicar of Wakefield?
Answer on page 146.

THE GREAT PRETENDERS

In 2004, as a counterpoint to the BBC survey of the nation's 100 favourite novels, John Walsh in *The Independent* asked his famous pals to do the exact opposite – to nominate the books they wished that they had never read. Here are some of the best, and most surprising:

The Lord of the Rings by JRR Tolkien
Anything about Gandalf, and those little things with hair between their toes. I hate that sort of portentous, phoney, medieval-magical way of writing.
Sir John Mortimer: Author and creator of Rumpole

Ulysses by James Joyce
I always failed to get very far with this. It's one of those books you think you ought to read because everyone says it's such a classic, but it's completely incomprehensible. I found it impenetrable and I got fed up with the style. It's been decades since I tried to read it, and I don't think I'll bother trying again.
Neil Hamilton: Disgraced former Conservative minister

The Harry Potter books by JK Rowling
I think they are absolute shit, just terrible, worse than Enid Blyton. I have discouraged my children from reading them. They are not particularly badly written – I don't mind bad writing – it's the smugness and the complicity with the reader that I dislike. It's like they're written by a focus group. JK Rowling is the sub-literary analogue of Tony Blair.
Jonathan Meades: Author and broadcaster

A Brief History of Time by Stephen Hawking
You think you understand it, but then you get to the end, and realise you don't.
Tony Banks: Labour MP for West Ham

LITERARY BANDWAGONS

McSweeneyites

A coterie of high-selling, high-fashion, post-ironic writers that has recently come begging to the halls of literary history, the McSweeneyites may still have a lot to prove. Spiritually led by American writer Dave Eggers, whose confessional first novel made him more money than he knew what to do with, it numbers Jonathan Safran Foer and British writers Zadie Smith and Nick Hornby among its members. Advocates of what they dub 'casualness' in writing, the McSweeneyites (named after Eggers' publishing firm) have been known to pepper their work with line drawings and visual gimmickry. Vastly successful, youthful and attractive, the McSweeneyites have faced criticism for being too insular and allowing the outlook of the group to stifle the imagination of the individual.

JOINING THE LIBRARY

Joining the library and borrowing books may be free, but it takes a bit of organisation to fill out the application card with all the necessary documents in hand. Here's what you'll need...

- proof of address (a bill less than three months old, a pension or benefit book)
- proof of signature (a credit card or passport)

Once you've joined, you can borrow from any of the city or borough's libraries and return loans to any branch. Children aged ten and under may borrow up to seven items; those aged 11 and over may borrow up to ten items.

WHAT A BIND

It all makes perfectly logical sense now, but there was a time when locating a book on the bookshelf was made more difficult by the absence of markings of any kind. The earliest printed books didn't show the title, author or any kind of design on their covers and, as a result, were shelved backwards with the spine at the back of the shelf and the pages facing out. Books were sold unbound in 'quires' (gatherings of printed sheets), which meant that if you wanted a bound book, you had to buy the quires and take them to your nearest bookbinder for binding in your choice of material.

POETIC PUZZLERS

Name the poet and poem from these famous lines...

1. A snake came to my water-trough

2. Bent double, like old beggars under sacks

3. Do not go gentle into that good night

4. Earth hath not anything to show more fair

5. How do I love thee? Let me count the ways

6. I met a traveller from an antique land

7. Macavity's a mystery cat: he's called the hidden paw

8. O my love's like a red, red rose

9. Quinquireme of Ninevah from distant Ophir

10. Season of mists and mellow fruitfulness

11. The curfew tolls the knell of parting day

12. Tyger! Tyger! burning bright

13. What is this life if, full of care

Answer on page 146.

STRANGE LIBRARY EXHIBITS

People leave the funniest things...

Charles Dickens' candleholder and pet raven (stuffed),
Free Library of Philadelphia

Guy Fawkes' gunpowder, British Library

Jeremy Bentham's embalmed corpse (with wax head),
University College London

A nineteenth-century Feng Shui Compass; a pencil made
by Henry David Thoreau; two teeth of a giant 'the size
of a fist'; a sixth-century BC Babylonian cylinder from
the reign of Nebuchadnezzar; an eighteenth-century
recipe To Dissolve a Cancer in the Breast;
Nathaniel Hawthorne's passport; pieces of Confederate
reconnaissance balloons made from ladies' dress silk;
a handbill announcing the abdication of Tsar Nicholas II;
and a 'Gay Monopoly' game,
New York Public Library

Roald Amundsen sledge from the Antarctica,
Australian State Library

DUMBING DOWN

The Penguin 'Good Booking' promotion sees the well-
reputed publishing house take something of a more low-
brow approach to book marketing. In order to 'make reading more attractive to young men', they launched a new
campaign in 2004 to 'make young men who read more
attractive to women'. Male readers are encouraged to visit
the Good Booking website (www.goodbooking.com),
which rates books using icons such as 'sex', 'nudity', 'kinky
sex', 'greed', 'drugs', 'fast cars' (that eternal winner) – and,
presumably, 'pull factor'. That's reverse psychology for you.

The Adventures of Huckleberry Finn, Mark Twain (1884)

Banned on racial grounds and by Concord Public Library as 'trash suitable only for the slums'. When Twain was asked to defend the charges, he replied: 'I am greatly troubled by what you say. I wrote Tom Sawyer and Huck Finn for adults exclusively, and it always distressed me when I find that boys and girls have been allowed access to them. The mind that becomes soiled in youth can never again be washed clean.' Needless to say, it needed a little more defending to avoid the ban.

Tropic of Cancer, Henry Miller (1934)

Banned until 1963 for sexual content and the use of a four-letter word beginning with 'c', the book was first released in France on condition that the cover contain an explicit warning to book buyers. The publishers printed the advisories... on removable dust jackets.

Madame Bovary, Gustave Flaubert (1857)

Banned on sexual grounds. Prosecutor Ernest Pinard put it succinctly: 'No gauze for him, no veils – he gives us nature in all her nudity and crudity.'

Ulysses, James Joyce (1922)

TS Eliot described it as 'a book to which we are all indebted, and from which none of us can escape', but this didn't stop it being banned on sexual grounds in the USA and the UK.

The Kama Sutra

Banned for its sexual content, this Hindu holy book has caused no end of trouble for censors.

Lady Chatterley's Lover, DH Lawrence (1928)

Rumour has it that Lawrence purposefully used sexually explicit language in an effort to raise the ire of the UK censors. It worked. The book was subject to obscenity trials up to the 1960s.

Pistis Sophia
Banned for heresy, it was a capital offence in Europe and Asia to own a copy for more than 1000 years.

The Satanic Verses, Salman Rushdie (1988)
Outlawed in Pakistan, Saudi Arabia, Egypt, Somalia, Sudan, Malaysia, Qatar, Indonesia, South Africa and India for its perceived criticism of Islam.

Frankenstein: a Modern Prometheus, Mary Shelley (1818)
Banned under South Africa's apartheid regime in 1955, for being 'indecent, objectionable, or obscene'. Anna Sewell's *Black Beauty* – a story about a horse – was also banned.

Lolita, Vladimir Nabokov (1955)
Nabokov broke one hell of a taboo when he published his now infamous 12th novel. It received a mixed response – Graham Greene considered it one of the best books of the year, while the *Daily Express* dismissed it as 'the filthiest book I've ever read'.

MALAPROPISMS

From *mal à propos* (French for inappropriate), the comical (and unintended) misuse of words was first brought to the stage by the self-educated Mrs Malaprop in Sheridan's 1775 Restoration comedy, *The Rivals*. Here are some of her best:

'...promise to forget this fellow – to illiterate him, I say, quite from your memory.' (obliterate)
'O, he will dissolve my mystery!' (resolve)
'He is the very pine-apple of politeness!' (pinnacle)
'I have since laid Sir Anthony's preposition before her.' (proposition)
'Why, murder's the matter! slaughter's the matter! killing's the matter! – but he can tell you the perpendiculars.' (particulars)

ALL-TIME TOP TEN BESTSELLERS

1. *The Bible* (c.1451–5)
2.5 billion copies sold in 2233 languages and dialects

2. *Quotations from the Works of Mao Tse-tung* (1966)
800 million; formerly known as *The Red Book*

3. *The Lord of the Rings, JRR Tolkien* (1954–55)
More than 100 million

4. *American Spelling Book*, Noah Webster (1783)
100 million

5. *The Guinness Book of Records* (now *Guinness World Records*, 1955)
More than 90 million

6. *World Almanac* (1868) 70 million

7. *The McGuffey Readers*, William Holmes McGuffey
(1836) 60 million

8. *The Common Sense Book of Baby and Child Care*,
Benjamin Spock (1946) More than 50 million

9. *A Message to Garcia*, Elbert Hubbard (1899)
Up to 40 million

10. *Valley of the Dolls*, Jacqueline Susann (1966)
More than 30 million

THE REWRITE WAS BETTER

Stupid White Pen
Michael Moore launches a blistering attack on
George W Bush's preferred writing utensil.

POETIC PUZZLERS

In Camus' *L'Etranger*, who was the stranger?
Answer on page 146.

POETIC PUZZLERS

Name the book and author of these famous –
and not-so-famous – opening lines.
Answers on page 146.

1. 1801 – I have just returned from a visit to my landlord
– the solitary neighbour that I shall be troubled with.

2. 'Christmas won't be Christmas without any presents,'
grumbled Jo, lying on the rug.

3. I am living at the Villa Borghese. There is not a crumb
of dirt anywhere nor a chair misplaced. We are alone here
and we are dead.

4. The boy with fair hair lowered himself down the last
few feet of rock and began to pick his way towards
the lagoon.

5. It was love at first sight.

6. What's it going to be then, eh?

7. 'To be born again,' sang Gibreel Farishta tumbling from
the heavens, 'first you have to die.'

8. On an exceptionally hot evening early in July a young
man came out of the garret in which he lodged in S. Place
and walked slowly, as though in hesitation, towards
K. bridge.

9. Mr Jones, of the Manor Farm, had locked the hen-house
for the night, but was too drunk to remember to shut
the popholes.

10. Happy families are all alike; every unhappy family
is unhappy in its own way.

PLAY-IT-SAFE NOM DE PLUME

Why risk your hard earned reputation just because you want to try something new? Here are some high-working authors who thought they'd play it on the safe side...

Amnesia Glasscock
John Steinbeck published *The Collected Poems* (1976) under this forgettable name.

Mary Westmacott
Agatha Christie tried her hand at gothic romances under this nom de plume, but the books – *Unfinished Portrait*, *The Rose and the Yew Tree* and *A Daughter's Daughter* – didn't attain anywhere near the fame of the writer's mysteries.

Jane Somers
Doris Lessing's *The Diaries* (1984) were published under this name.

Richard Bachman
When Stephen King released *Thinner* (1984) under the pseudonym Richard Bachman, one literary review described the book as 'what Stephen King would write like, if Stephen King could really write'. There were plenty of red faces when the 'real' author was revealed.

Victoria Lucas
Sylvia Plath released her only novel, *The Bell Jar*, under this assumed name.

Robert Markham
The penname Kingsley Amis used for his James Bond novel *Colonel Sun* (1968).

Alcofri bas Nasier
François Rabelais created his penname out of an anagram of his own name to release the classic *Gargantua and Pantagruel*.

CHINESE WHISPERS

Seasoned quoters take heed, you may not be half as accurate as you think you are...

Commonly: Alas, poor Yorick, I knew him well
Actually: Alas poor Yorick! I knew him, Horatio
Shakespeare, *Hamlet*

Commonly: Accidents will happen
Actually: Accidents will occur
Charles Dickens, *David Copperfield* (1849–1850)

Commonly: Water, water everywhere, but not a drop to drink
Water, water everywhere, nor e'er a drop to drink
Water, water everywhere, and not a drop to drink
Actually: Water, water everywhere, nor any drop to drink
Samuel Taylor Coleridge, *Rime of the Ancient Mariner* (1798)

Commonly: A blessing in disguise
Actually: Blessings in disguise
James Hervey, *Reflections on a Flower Garden* (1746)

Commonly: Hell hath no fury like a woman scorned
Actually: Heaven has no rage like love to hatred turned
Nor hell a fury like a woman scorned
William Congreve, *The Mourning Bride* (1697)

Commonly: Money is the root of all evil
Actually: For the love of money is the root of all evil
The Bible, Timothy 6:10

Commonly: Adding fuel to the fire
Actually: Adding fuel to the flame
John Milton, *Samson Agonistes* (1671)

Commonly: Ask me no questions, and I'll tell you no lies
Actually: Ask me no questions, and I'll tell you no fibs
Oliver Goldsmith, *She Stoops to Conquer* (1774)

POETIC PUZZLERS

How many novels did the Brontë sisters write?
Answer on page 147.

NOT IN THEIR LIFETIME

Success is sweet, but sometimes it can come that little
bit too late...

The Collected Poems – Sylvia Plath (1981)
Plath's Pulitzer Prize-winning collected works were
published 18 years after her death in 1963.

The Leopard – Giuseppe Tomaso di Lampedusa (1958)
When the Sicilian nobleman Giuseppe Tomaso di
Lampedusa died in 1957, he left the completed (and previ-
ously rejected) manuscript of *The Leopard* in his drawer. It
was published shortly after and quickly became a success.

Unpublished Poems – Emily Dickinson (1935)
Comparatively unnoticed during her lifetime, Dickinson's
poetry was published posthumously to instant success,
transforming her from a 'forgotten poetess' to 'the greatest
American poet of the nineteenth century' almost overnight.

Poems – Dante Rossetti (1870)
When his wife died, Rossetti decided to bury his manuscript of poems with her. Seven years later he changed his
mind, so he disinterred the poems and had them published
to great acclaim.

Pensées – Blaise Pascal (1670)
In *Pensées*, Pascal tried to answer that all-important
question – why are we here? – but didn't manage to get it
out in his own lifetime.

Harry Potter uses *The Standard Book of Spells* by Miranda Goshawk in the JK Rowling children's books.

The Duke's Daughter was written by central character Jo March in Louisa May Alcott's *Little Women*. The money she made went to pay the butcher's bill.

On the Polyphonic Motets of Lassus, *On the Surface Anatomy of the Human Ear* and *Upon the Uses of Dogs in the Work of the Detective* are all the imaginary brainchildren of Arthur Conan Doyle's Sherlock Holmes.

Well, that about wraps it up for God, *Where God Went Wrong*, *Some More of God's Greatest Mistakes* and *Who is this God Person Anyway?* by Oolon Colluphid are all referred to in Douglas Adams' *A Hitchhiker's Guide to the Galaxy*. Adams explains Oolon's grudge against God in an episode where his pregnant mother is given a fright by a pair of Jehovah's witnesses.

Protagonist Humbert Humbert writes *Lolita, or the Confession of a White Widowed Male* in Vladimir Nabokov's *Lolita*.

Bilbo Baggins works on *The Red Book of Westmarch* (aka *The Red Book of Periannath*) in JRR Tolkien's *The Hobbit* and *The Lord of the Rings*.

Speculations on the Source of the Hampstead Ponds, With some Observations on the Theory of Tittlebats is the literary construction of Samuel Pickwick in Charles Dickens' novel *The Pickwick Papers*.

Milo Temesvar's *On the Use of Mirrors in the Game of Chess* is referred to in Umberto Eco's *The Name of the Rose* and De Amicis' *Chronicles of the Zodiac* in Eco's *Foucault's Pendulum* despite the fact that neither the books nor their authors exist.

Is *Man a Myth?*, *Men, Monks and Gamekeepers: a Study in Popular Legend* and *The Life and Letters of Silenus* are all to be found in Mr Tumnus' cave in *The Lion, the Witch and the Wardrobe*.

The works of fictional Victorian poets Randolph Henry Ash and Christabel LaMotte guide the story of the real-life novel *Possession: A Romance*, by AS Byatt.

Advanced Ass-licking for Graduate Students, *The Proper Method of Farting in Company*, *The Law's Codpiece* and *How to Keep it up until You're Ninety* (among others) appear in Rabelais' *Gargantua and Pantagruel*.

Fictional alter-ego Kilgore Trout creates the science fiction works of *The Gospel from Outer Space*, *Venus on the Half-Shell*, and *Now it can be Told* in Kurt Vonnegut's series of books.

NOVELTY POP

Celebrity meets children's literature...

Madonna – *The English Roses* (2003)
Prince Charles – *The Old Man of Lochnagar* (1980)
Sarah Ferguson – *Budgie the Helicopter* (1989)
Bill Cosby – *The Meanest Thing to Say* (1997)
Jamie Lee Curtis – *Today I Feel Silly and Other Moods that Make My Day* (1998), *Tell Me Again About the Night I Was Born* (1999), *When I Was Little: A Four-Year-Old's Memoir of her Youth* (1995) and *Where Do Balloons Go? An Uplifting Mystery* (2000)
Mary Chapin Carpenter – *Halley Came to Jackson* (1990)
Jimmy Carter – *The Little Baby Snoogle-Fleejer* (1995)
Sophie Dahl – *The Man With the Dancing Eyes* (2003)

ON HER MAJESTY'S SEQUEL SERVICE

Absurd plots, sexist dialogue and dirty villains: when Ian Fleming's Bond charmed his way onto the page, the nation was hooked and Hollywood followed soon after. But when Fleming died in 1964, someone had to take over the literary reins...

Kingsley Amis (under the pseudonym Robert Markham):
Colonel Sun (1968)

John Gardner (the official Bond sequel writer):
Licence Renewed (1981), *For Special Services* (1982),
Icebreaker (1983), *Role of Honour* (1984),
Nobody Lives Forever (1986), *No Deals, Mr Bond*
(1987), *Scorpius* (1987), *Win Lose or Die* (1989),
Licence to Kill (1989), *Brokenclaw* (1990),
The Man From Barbarossa (1991),
Death is Forever (1992), *Never Send Flowers* (1993),
SeaFire (1994), *Golden Eye* (1995), *Cold* (1996)

Raymond Benson:
Zero Minus Ten (1997), *Tomorrow Never Dies* (1997),
The Facts of Death (1998), *High Time to Kill* (1999),
The World is not Enough (1999), *Doubleshot* (2000),
Never Dream of Dying (2001),
The Man with the Red Tattoo (2002),
Die Another Day (2002)

POETIC PUZZLERS

In HG Wells' *The Invisible Man*, who was
the invisible man?
Answer on page 147.

COULD HAVE BEEN CALLED?

As You Like It – Like You Enjoy It
Catch-22 – Trap XXII
The Cat in the Hat – The Feline in the Cap
The God of Small Things – The Deity of Tiny Objects
Great Expectations – Huge Hopes
The Green Mile – The Emerald Kilometre
Little Women – Mini Females
The Lord of the Rings – The God of the Bands
The Old Man and the Sea – The OAP and the Ocean
The Time Machine – The Occasion Contraption
100 Years of Solitude – Ten Decades of Loneliness

LITERARY PAY OFFS

When celebrated British novelist Fay Weldon brokered a deal in 2001 with Italian jewellery maker Bulgari to plug their products in her novel appropriately entitled *The Bulgari Collection*, the literary world was up in arms. But Weldon wasn't the last novelist to accept cash for product placement in fiction. In 2004, Ford paid British novelist Carole Matthews an undisclosed (but allegedly five-digit) sum in return for featuring the Ford Fiesta in her next two novels. But Matthews dismissed claims it was a sell out: 'Wherever my heroine is driving a car, it will now be a Ford Fiesta,' she told the BBC's World Business Report. 'That's the only thing they've asked me to do, they've placed no other constraints on my writing at all.

WHEN EDITORS GET IT WRONG

When Andre Bernard was researching rejection letters for *Rotten Rejections: The Letters that Publishers Wish They'd Never Sent*, he came across some howlers....

'The author of this book is beyond psychiatric help.'
Crash by J G Ballard

'This will set publishing back 25 years.'
The Deer Park by Norman Mailer

'Do you realize, young woman, that you're the first American writer ever to poke fun at sex.'
Gentlemen Prefer Blondes by Anita Loos

'The girl doesn't, it seems to me, have a special perception or feeling which would lift that book above the "curiosity" level.'
The Diary of Anne Frank

'The grand defect of the work, I think, as a work of art is the low-mindedness and vulgarity of the chief actors. There is hardly a "lady" or "gentleman" amongst them.'
Barchester Towers by Anthony Trollope

'We are not interested in science fiction which deals with negative utopias. They do not sell.'
Carrie by Stephen King

'I haven't really the foggiest idea about what the man is trying to say... Apparently the author intends it to be funny – possibly even satire – but it is really not funny on any intellectual level... From your long publishing experience you will know that it is less disastrous to turn down a work of genius than to turn down talented mediocrities.'
Catch-22 by Joseph Heller

'You're welcome to le Carré – he hasn't got any future.'
The Spy who Came in from the Cold by John le Carré

'It is impossible to sell animal stories in the USA'
Animal Farm by George Orwell

BOOKS TO BRAWL TO

Among the Thugs, Bill Buford (2001)
The Bad Guys Won! A Season of Brawling, Bimbo Chasing, and *Championship Baseball with Straw, Doc, Mookie, Nails, the Kid, and the Rest of the 1986 Mets*, Jeff Pearlman (2004)
The Bear, William Faulkner (1942)
Bloody Casuals: Diary of a Football Hooligan, Jay Allan (1989)
Fat City, Leonard Gardner (1996)
Fight Club, Chuck Palahniuk (1996)
Glue, by Irvine Welsh (2001)
The Illiad, Homer
Homer describes every blow struck by every soldier...
Raging Bull: My Story, Jake La Motta (1997)
Reservoir Dogs, Quentin Tarantino (2000)
Snatch: The Shooting Script, Guy Ritchie (2001)
The Three Musketeers, Alexandre Dumas (1844)
A Violent Life, Pier Paolo Pasolini (1996)

BOOK CLUB FAVOURITES

Every year Reading Group Choices announce the most read books of the previous year in book clubs across the US. Here are the top picks from 2003:

The Secret Life of Bees, Sue Monk Kidd
The Da Vinci Code, Dan Brown
The Red Tent, Anita Diamant
Seabiscuit: An American Legend, Laura Hillenbrand
Life of Pi, Yann Martel
Girl with a Pearl Earring, Tracy Chevalier
Peace Like a River, Leif Enger
Bel Canto, Ann Patchett
The Lovely Bones, Alice Sebold
Empire Falls, Richard Russo

BOOK IN BOOK READING

Books in which protagonists read...

David Copperfield, Charles Dickens

Gone with the Wind, Margaret Mitchell.
Melanie reads Dickens aloud to a group of women
tensely awaiting word of their men out on
a vigilante mission.

Jane Eyre, Charlotte Brontë

Madame Bovary, Gustave Flaubert
The potentially misleading influence of romantic fiction
is brought to life in Flaubert's Emma Bovary.

Swallows and Amazons, Arthur Ransome
All the children, but especially the sensitive protagonist
Titty Walker, adore *Robinson Crusoe*.

The Never Ending Story, Stephen B Grant

To Kill a Mockingbird, Harper Lee
Jem is forced to read each day to a dying old woman
who is trying to break her addiction to morphine.

Northanger Abbey, Jane Austen
Austen charts a young woman's reading habits
and the impact on her character.

POETIC PUZZLERS

Who am I?
C
RAD
Answer on page 147.

BOOKSHOP STORIES

Shakespeare & Co
Two bookshops, two movements, one spirit...

In 1921, Sylvia Beach founded Shakespeare & Co at 12, rue de l'Odeon, Paris, and through it introduced writers Ernest Hemingway and F Scott Fitzgerald to European readers. As well as providing a meeting place for the collection of writers who would become known as the Lost Generation, Beach sealed her shop's place in literary history by agreeing to publish James Joyce's *Ulysses*, then regarded by publishing houses as little more than pornographic filth. Needless to say the gamble paid off.

In 1941, with Paris under Nazi occupation, Shakespeare & Co was threatened with closure when Beach refused to sell a copy of *Finnegan's Wake* to a German officer. Rather than risk the destruction of her stock, Beach mobilised her friends and in the two hours it took the officer to return, all trace of the bookshop had vanished.

Twenty-three years later, George Whitman, the owner of a bookshop at 37, rue de la Bûcherie, sought Beach's permission to resurrect her company's name and spirit. With permission granted, Whitman continued his commitment to writers by installing beds among the books, thereby providing the accommodation that can still be enjoyed today. In exchange for his hospitality, Whitman (now in his nineties and an enigmatic character who singes his hair shorter with the flame of a candle) asks only for an hour of work per day and a commitment to match his prolific reading habits.

LITERARY CLUBS OF OLD LONDON

The Kit-Cat Club (est. 1700)
This club's earliest meetings were held in a tavern on Chancery Lane kept by Christopher Cat (hence the name). One of the club's customs was to toast the era's beauties in verse, which were afterwards engraved on the club glasses. The Earl of Halifax and Sir Samuel Garth were the most prolific contributors to the club's literature, being responsible for 13 toasts between them.

The Blue Stocking Club (est. 1925)
This women's club was founded by Elizabeth Robinson, wife of Edward Montagu as a 'discussion party', which saw such illustrious guests as Horace Walpole, Dr Johnson, Burke, Garrick and other late eighteenth-century literati.

The (Literary) Club (est. 1764)
This popular club boasted members that included Dr Johnson (hence its other title, Dr Johnson's Club), Edward Burke, Oliver Goldsmith and, later, Tennyson, Gladstone and Lord Salisbury. Its membership was limited to 40. Entry was decided by an anonymous vote which included the 'one black ball will exclude' rule popular among clubs over the ages.

HITLER'S FORGOTTEN LIBRARY

Some of the books from Adolf Hitler's personal library are now housed in the rare-book reading room of the Library of Congress. Among the 1200 books can be found...

Don Quixote, Miguel de Cervantes
Gulliver's Travels, Jonathan Swift
Mein Kampf, Adolf Hitler
Robinson Crusoe, Daniel Defoe
The Predictions of Nostradamus
Uncle Tom's Cabin, Harriet Beecher Stowe

A BRIEF HISTORY OF BRAILLE

Parisian Louis Braille invented the Braille reading system nearly 200 years ago at the age of 15 when attending the Royal Institution for Blind Youth.

French army captain, Charles Barbier de la Serre, had invented the basic technique of using raised dots for tactile writing and reading to allow soldiers to compose and read messages at night without light. Barbier presented his system (Sonography) to the Institution for Blind Youth, hoping that it would be officially adopted there. Braille discovered both the potential of the basic idea and the shortcomings and within three years had developed the system that we know today as Braille, which employs a six-dot 'cell', or character based on normal spelling.

Each Braille cell is made up of six dot positions, which are arranged in a rectangle comprising two columns of three dots. A dot may be raised at any of the six positions, and in any combination. Counting the space – where no dots are raised – there are 64 combinations.

Louis Braille published the first Braille book in 1829. In 1837, he added symbols for maths and music. Today, in virtually every language around the world, the code named after Louis Braille is the standard form of writing and reading used by blind people.

LITERARY PARODIES

Ripped-off titles

Of Mice and Men (John Steinbeck, 1937)
Of Mycenae and Men (a BBC2 sitcom starring Diana Dors broadcast in March 1979)

Who's afraid of Virginia Woolf? (Edward Albee, 1962)
Me, I'm afraid of Virginia Woolf (The first of Alan Bennett's Six Plays, broadcast on ITV in December 1978)

Walden, or Life in the Woods (Henry David Thoreau, 1854)
Walden Two (Burrhus Frederik Skinner, 1948)

Portrait of the Artist as a Young Man (James Joyce, 1914)
Portrait of the Artist as a Young Dog (Dylan Thomas, 1920)

The Silmarillion (JRR Tolkien, 1977)
The Sellamillion: The Disappointing 'Other' Book (ARRR Roberts, 2004)

Eats, Shoots & Leaves: The Zero Tolerance Approach to Punctuation (Lynne Truss, 2003)
Eats, Shites and Leaves: Crap English and How to Use it (A Parody, 2004)

Harry Potter books, JK Rowling
Barry Trotter and the Shameless Parody (Michael Gerber, 2002), *Barry Trotter and the Unnecessary Sequel* (Michael Gerber, 2003), *Barry Trotter and the Dead Horse* (Michael Gerber, 2004)

Lord of the Rings (JRR Tolkien, 1954–1955)
Bored of the Rings (Harvard National Lampoon, 1969)

LITERARY HOARDERS

The earliest-known collection of reading materials – a series of clay tablets – was established in ancient Mesopotamia 5000 years ago. Archaeologists also uncovered a store of papyrus scrolls from 1300–1200 BC in the ancient Egyptian cities of Amarna and Thebes and thousands of clay tablets in the palace of King Sennacherib, Assyrian ruler from 704–681BC, at Nineveh, his capital city.

The first private library is attributed to Aristotle. Ancient geographer Strabo reported that Aristotle 'was the first to have put together a collection of books and to have taught the kings in Egypt how to arrange a library'. As a result of his instructions, the first public library was opened in Alexandria in 330 BC.

In the early 500s, Pachomius established a monastery in Egypt, at which literacy was compulsory. This saw theological libraries spring up all over the monastic world.

Theological collections grew side by side with royal libraries. France's national library, the Bibliothèque Nationale de France, began life in 1367 as the Royal Library of Charles V.

The earliest public library in the UK was associated with London's Guild Hall in 1425. A second opened in Edinburgh in 1580.

Sir Thomas Bodley rebuilt the Duke of Gloucester's library at Oxford in the late 1500s. It was renamed the Bodleian Library, and today is the second largest in the country, behind the British Library, which was founded in 1759 as part of the British Museum.

Once British Parliament passed the Public Library Act in 1850, libraries began to spread throughout the nation. Today, 58% of Britons are library members, borrowing some 480 million books a year.

DURING THE COMPILATION OF THIS BOOK, THE COMPANION TEAM...

Added an extra 17 feet of bookshelves to their homes

Fell asleep in nine different libraries

Read *Ulysses* from cover to cover and prepared eloquent discourse on the Joycean perspective

Thought they saw Martin Amis at Heathrow airport once, but he was a long way off, and his back was turned, and come to think of it he looked a little tall, so in retrospect it might have been someone else

Worked out that the average novel length among those they had read was 273 pages and 17 words

Read tonnes of sonnet anthologies, then realised that the two words are anagrams of each other

Wondered if any poet had ever been more aptly named than Wordsworth

Read Pincher Martin, only to find the last page was missing

Started to write a very good short story, but couldn't decide which word to use at the

Figured that if a Grecian Urns enough, then it doesn't matter what he's Ode

Bought 11 first editions off ebay

Lied about the *Ulysses* thing

Please note that although every effort has been made to ensure accuracy in this book, the above statistics may be the result of tall-tale-telling minds.

POETIC PUZZLERS

The answers. As if you needed them.

P14   Thomas Hardy, Emily Brontë, TS Eliot and Edgar Allan Poe

P21   The authors are all thought to have had careers as spies.

P28   They all set novels in trains: *Murder on the Orient Express* (Agatha Christie), *The Great Train Robbery* (Michael Crichton), *Stamboul Train* (Graham Greene) and *The Railway Children* (E Nesbit).

P40   They have all appeared in cameo roles in the film adaptations of their books: JG Ballard (*Empire of the Sun*), Robert Harling (*Steel Magnolias*), Stephen King (*Pet Cemetery*, among others) and Irvine Welsh (*Trainspotting*).

P44   Myshkin

P72   Although usually associated with the Queen in *Alice's Adventures in Wonderland*, the phrase actually originated in Shakespeare's *Richard III* (Act III, scene iv) when Richard of Gloucester (as he was then) sentenced Lord Hastings to death with the words: 'Thou art a traitor: off with his head!'

P90   Sarah Woodruff

P92   WB Yeats

P101   Oliver Mellors

P107   *David Copperfield*. In 1868 he wrote: 'Of all my books, I like this the best. It will be easily believed that I am a fond parent of every child of my fancy, and that no one can ever love a family as dearly as I love them. But, like many fond parents, I have in my heart of hearts a favourite child. And his name is *David Copperfield*.'

P113 Antonio

P119 Dr Charles Primrose

P122 1. 'Snake', DH Lawrence

2. 'Dulce et Decorum Est', Willfred Owen

3. 'Do Not Go Gentle Into That Good Night', Dylan Thomas

4. 'Composed Upon Westminster Bridge', William Wordsworth

5. Sonnet 42: 'How do I love thee? Let me count the ways', Elizabeth Barrett Browning

6. 'Ozymandias of Egypt', Percy Bysshe Shelley

7. 'Macavity: The Mystery Cat', TS Eliot

8. 'A Red, Red Rose', Robert Burns

9. 'Cargoes', John Masefield

10. 'Ode To Autumn', John Keats

11. 'Elegy Written in a Country Churchyard', Thomas Gray

12. 'The Tyger', William Blake

13. 'Leisure', WH Daview

P127 Mersault

P128 1. *Wuthering Heights*, Emily Brontë (1845–1847)

2. *Little Women*, Louisa May Alcott (1868–1869)

3. *Tropic of Cancer*, Henry Miller (1934)

4. *Lord of the Flies*, William Golding (1954)

5. *Catch-22*, Joseph Heller (1961)

6. *A Clockwork Orange*, Anthony Burgess (1962)

7. *The Satanic Verses*, Salman Rushdie (1988)

8. *Crime and Punishment*, Dostoevsky (1866)

9. *Animal Farm*, George Orwell (1945)

10. *Anna Karenina*, Leo Tolstoy (1873-7)

P131   Seven: *Agnes Grey* and *The Tenant of Wildfell Hall* (Anne); *The Professor*, *Jane Eyre*, *Shirley* and *Villette* (Charlotte); and *Wuthering Heights* (Emily).

P134   Griffin

P138   (Joseph) Conrad

LITERARY NOTES AND MUSINGS

LITERARY NOTES AND MUSINGS

LITERARY NOTES AND MUSINGS

LITERARY NOTES AND MUSINGS

LITERARY NOTES AND MUSINGS

LITERARY NOTES AND MUSINGS

LITERARY NOTES AND MUSINGS

LITERARY NOTES AND MUSINGS

LITERARY NOTES AND MUSINGS

LITERARY NOTES AND MUSINGS

LITERARY NOTES AND MUSINGS

LITERARY NOTES AND MUSINGS